PENGUIN

The Jung

Rudyard Joseph Kipling was born in Bombay in 1865. His father, John Lockwood Kipling, was the author and illustrator of *Beast and Man in India* and his mother, Alice, was the sister of Lady Burne-Jones. In 1871 Kipling was brought home from India and spent five unhappy years with a foster family in Southsea, an experience he later drew on in *The Light That Failed* (1891). The years he spent at the United Services College, a school for officers' children, are depicted in *Stalky & Co.* (1899) and the character of Beetle is something of a self-portrait. It was during his time at the college that he began writing poetry and *Schoolboy Lyrics* was published privately in 1881. In the following year he started work as a journalist in India and, while there, produced a body of work, stories, sketches and poems – notably *Plain Tales from the Hills* (1888) – which made him an instant literary celebrity when he returned to England in 1889. *Barrack-Room Ballads* (1892) contains some of his most popular pieces, including 'Mandalay', 'Gunga Din' and 'Danny Deever'. In this collection Kipling experimented with form and dialect, notably the cockney accent of the soldier poems, but the influence of hymns, music-hall songs, ballads and public poetry can be found throughout his verse.

In 1892 he married an American, Caroline Balestier, and from 1892 to 1896 they lived in Vermont, where Kipling wrote *The Jungle Book*, published in 1894. In 1901 came *Kim* and in 1902 the *Just So Stories*. Tales of every kind – including historical and science fiction – continued to flow from his pen, but *Kim* is generally thought to be his greatest long work, putting him high among the chroniclers of British expansion.

From 1902 Kipling made his home in Sussex, but he continued to travel widely and caught his first glimpse of warfare in South Africa, where he reported on the Boer War. However, many of the views he expressed were rejected by anti-imperialists, who accused him of jingoism and love of violence. Though rich and successful, he never again enjoyed the literary esteem of his early years. With the onset of the Great War, his work became more sombre. The stories he subsequently wrote, *A Diversity of Creatures* (1917), *Debits and Credits* (1926) and *Limits and*

Renewals (1932), are now thought by many to contain some of his finest writing. The death of his only son in 1915 also contributed to a new inwardness of vision.

Kipling refused to accept the role of Poet Laureate and other civil honours, but he was the first English writer to be awarded the Nobel Prize, in 1907. He died in 1936 and his autobiographical fragment *Something of Myself* was published the following year.

Thomas Pinney is William M. Keck Distinguished Service Professor of English, Emeritus, at Pomona College, California, and was chair of the department before his retirement. In addition to editing Kipling's letters, he is editor of the essays of George Eliot and the letters of Thomas Babington Macaulay, and the author of *A History of Wine in America*.

RUDYARD KIPLING

The Jungle Play

Edited with an Introduction and Notes by
THOMAS PINNEY

PENGUIN BOOKS

PENGUIN BOOKS

Published by the Penguin Group
Penguin Books Ltd, 27 Wrights Lane, London w8 5TZ, England
Penguin Putnam Inc., 375 Hudson Street, New York, New York 10014, USA
Penguin Books Australia Ltd, Ringwood, Victoria, Australia
Penguin Books Canada Ltd, 10 Alcorn Avenue, Toronto, Ontario, Canada M4V 3B2
Penguin Books India (P) Ltd, 11, Community Centre, Panchsheel Park, New Delhi – 110 017, India
Penguin Books (NZ) Ltd, Private Bag 102902, NSMC, Auckland, New Zealand
Penguin Books (South Africa) (Pty) Ltd, 5 Watkins Street, Denver Ext 4, Johannesburg 2094, South Africa

Penguin Books Ltd, Registered Offices: Harmondsworth, Middlesex, England

First published by Allen Lane The Penguin Press 2000
Published in Penguin Classics 2001
1

Printed in England by Clays Ltd, St Ives plc

Contents

List of Illustrations

Introduction

The Jungle Play is a new work by Rudyard Kipling, written evidently
with serious intent for performance and publication, and then put
away and forgotten for a century. It is a dramatic version of certain
stories appearing in *The Jungle Book* (1894) and *The Second Jungle
Book* (1895). It is thus a derivative rather than a wholly new work.
But it is different enough, in form and substance, from its originals
to make a fresh addition to the canon of a great writer's creations.
The story of its origins, its disappearance and its rediscovery is set
forth in the first part of this introduction.

The Evidence for Attribution

The first reference that we have to something called a 'Jungle Play'
occurs in Mrs Kipling's diary for 15 November 1900: 'Rud works
on his Jungle play.'[1] A few weeks later, writing to his old Vermont
friend Dr James Conland at the end of 1900, Kipling told him: 'Just
now I've been putting the Jungle Book into the form of a play,
which may or may not be acted next year.'[2] The remark that it 'may
or may not be acted next year' suggests that a definite production
had been in mind from the beginning, and it is possible that the
idea of dramatizing the *Jungle Books* originated in response to
the request of a theatrical producer. But that is only a guess. In
summarizing the year 1900 at the end of his abstract of Mrs Kipling's
diary for that year, Douglas Rees wrote: 'Towards the end of the
year [Kipling] devoted a lot of time to a Jungle Play, Jungle Lance.'

If Kipling in fact thought of the dramatic version as 'Jungle Lance', it is hard to see why, since Mowgli carries only a knife. But it is interesting to learn from Rees, who was one of the few to see Mrs Kipling's complete diary before its destruction, that Kipling 'devoted a lot of time' to the play, under whatever name.

The next reference to the play occurs six months later, in the other extant abstract of Mrs Kipling's diary, that made by Kipling's biographer, Charles Carrington. The entry for 18 June 1901 reads: 'Rud working on a Jungle Book play.' The equivalent entry in the Rees abstract is a summary under the date of 25 June 1901: 'Rud works on Jungle play (and a number of subsequent days).' On 5 July 1901 Kipling informed his mother-in-law, Anna Smith Balestier, that 'I have rewritten my jungle play and some theatrical big bugs seem to think a lot of it.'[3]

These references are the only external evidence we have for the existence and date of Kipling's dramatic version of *The Jungle Book*, but they are sufficiently distinct. They show that it was a thing that he not merely thought of doing, or for which he might have received a commission: it was actually written, and then rewritten over a period of more than half a year. Kipling's language implies that the work was complete: one does not 'rewrite' a fragment. He may have had a particular producer in mind from the outset, but in any case the script had attracted the interest of 'some theatrical big bugs', either in its first version or in its revised version, by the middle of 1901. Kipling certainly seems to have been working with the idea of making a play that would in fact be produced.[4]

But then nothing more is heard of it. There are no further references in the letters, or in the surviving forms of Mrs Kipling's diary, and, so far as I know, no mention is made of it in the considerable anecdotal literature about Kipling and his work. Only the relatively few who have had a chance to read Kipling's letters and to consult the surviving extracts from Mrs Kipling's diary would even have heard of *The Jungle Play*. And if any one of those few had paused to wonder what had happened to *The Jungle Play* the conclusion would have been that it must have joined that considerable number of Kipling's rejected works of which we read in his letters and in his autobiography, *Something of Myself*. The list includes the early novel called 'Mother Maturin', the volume of stories and sketches to be called 'The Book of the Forty-Five Mornings', the discarded stories that he wrote for *Puck of Pook's Hill* and *Rewards and Fairies*, and the poem that he wrote on American affairs after the First World War, 'Ed Baker'. All of these, and a great many more, Kipling determined for one reason or another not to publish. Moreover, he seems to have destroyed the manuscripts: at least, no one has yet found any trace of these works.

The Jungle Play, however, was not destroyed. Why it was not produced no one can now say, but it is easy enough to imagine all sorts of reasons, most of them to do with the speculative and uncertain character of theatrical production in general. As Kipling said: 'plays are like fishing. There's any amount of tackle and bait and very poor results.'[5] Whatever the decision of the theatrical big bugs may have been as to the chances of Kipling's play, Kipling himself did not think so poorly of it as to destroy the manuscript. Instead, it seems to have remained quietly among his papers until they passed into the care of the University of Sussex Library. That was after the death in 1976 of Kipling's only surviving child, Mrs Elsie Bambridge, a childless widow, who left her estate to the National Trust: with this bequest was included the great collection of papers – financial, literary, domestic – belonging to Kipling, his wife, and his daughter. The Trust, in turn, deposited the Kipling papers in the University of Sussex Library, and there they were catalogued, very skilfully and usefully, by the librarian then in charge of special collections, John Burt.

When, in the course of working his way through the mass of papers left by Mrs Bambridge, John Burt came to the typescript of *The Jungle Play*, he had no information about its origins other than what might be deduced from its presence among Kipling's papers and from the fact that it bore a number of corrections in what might be Kipling's own hand. There were, however, other adaptations of Kipling's work among those papers that clearly were not the work of Kipling: an undated 'photo-dramatization' called 'The Gate of the Hundred Sorrows';[6] a dramatization of *The Jungle*

Book called 'Mowgli', dated 1939; and a film script for *Soldiers Three*, probably from 1934 to 1935, when Kipling was collaborating on, or making suggestions for, a script of the soldier tales for Gaumont.[7] Confronted with this mixed bag, Burt rightly exercised caution and entered *The Jungle Play* in the catalogue of the Kipling Papers at Sussex under the heading of 'Adaptations of Works by Kipling', adding a question by way of note: 'with manuscript corrections by R. K.?'.

A good many people who have worked on the Kipling Papers in recent years have seen *The Jungle Play* in the list of titles at Sussex, and some of them, including me, must actually have looked at it at some point during those years, without tumbling to what it was they were seeing. My moment of illumination came in March of 1998, when I was preparing a talk to be given at Magdalene College, Cambridge. Kipling had been made an honorary fellow of Magdalene in 1932, a distinction of which he was particularly proud. After his death, Mrs Kipling established a fellowship in his memory at Magdalene, and it was at the invitation of the current holder of the Kipling fellowship, Dr Jeffery Lewins, that I had prepared my talk. I took as my topic an imaginary bibliography of Kipling, a bibliography that would list those works that Kipling thought about writing but did not write, or that he wrote but did not publish, or that he published but did not collect. The 'lost' *Jungle Play* would naturally figure in such a list. I had therefore reviewed the evidence about *The Jungle Play* and had it still fresh in mind when, just before giving my talk at Magdalene, I paid a brief visit to the Kipling Papers at the University of Sussex Library. I had some quite unrelated questions to inquire into, but my eye was caught by the catalogue entry for *The Jungle Play*.[8]

I sent for it, meaning to examine it attentively for the first time. What I found was a typescript of some eighty-five pages,[9] bearing a great many corrections and additions in ink. I was at once struck by the evidence of the manuscript corrections. They were undoubtedly in Kipling's holograph, and they consisted almost entirely of detailed corrections of expression – deletions, additions, alterations – such as a man lavishes only on his own text. And they

We do not get ~~a~~ full gorge every night~~?~~ ^(Take) ~~T~~he Bull! The bull!

AKELA. Look well, O Wolves!

BAGH. Do ye take my price, Free Hunters?

WOL. We take the price. We will accept the man-cub to run with us in the pack, as a free hunter under the moon. . . ~~Now~~ let us get to our gorge! The bull! The bull!

MONKEYS. And the Free People call us greedy! ~~Well, this is what we'll~~ ~~do——we must go later. We ought to have belonged to us.~~ Come ~~along,~~ ^(brothers!) and we'll ~~make fun at~~ ^(mock) them ~~as~~ ^(while) they eat the ^(a) bull.

 (Exeunt Wolves, all except Mother Wolf and Akela).

BAL. That was well done, ~~man's cub only.~~ I do not love killing - I.

SH. KH. (to Bagh.) Good hunting, Black Cat of the Jungle. Thou hast cheated me of my meat.

BAGH. Thy meat, Painted Butcher of man. Then why didst thou not kill the thing when ye first ~~met it~~ ^(found it)

TAB. My noble master had previously lamed his foot.

M. WOLF. I gave him leave if he would first kill me. I was ready for the fight. He knows it. He was afraid.

SH. KH. Come away, Tabaqui. Those who bathe in dirty water must expect a soiled ~~skin.~~ ^(coat) Another time I will kill first and talk later. Let the man-cub and his ~~friends beware.~~ ^(pack look) ~~to it.~~

 (Exit SHERE KHAN and TABAQUI).

BAL. ~~They are~~ very well matched - a lame tiger and a lying jackal.

BAGH. Let them go. If I know anything of man this naked cub will some day make Shere Khan to roar to another tune. Men are very wise - eh, Akela?

Facsimile of a page from the typescript of
The Jungle Play

were in the form that Kipling describes as his preferred method in his account of his working procedures in *Something of Myself*.[10] Lines and phrases to be altered had been inked out with a brush, and the additions or changes added, in pen and ink, in Kipling's hand. The combination of Kipling's references to a 'Jungle Play' with a carefully corrected typescript of an actual *Jungle Play* among his papers seemed to me decisive even before I read the play itself.

As I did, my conviction grew beyond any doubt. Of course the language of the play, much of it, is taken directly from the text of the *Jungle Books*. But there is a good deal of new material, too, not only in prose but in verse, and in adapting the mixed description and dialogue of the *Jungle Books* to dramatic form, a constant process of altering and adapting has gone on. Does the result sound like Kipling? I think so. It is of course notoriously difficult, if not impossible, to prove on the basis of style – that is, the habits of a writer's language – that a literary work *must* have been written by a particular author; and it is equally difficult to prove the opposite – that it could *not* have been written by a particular author. So I will not labour the argument for Kipling's authorship on a stylistic basis, knowing that it would persuade only the converted. By far the greater part of the alterations made to the text are of a kind that attend to emphasis, nuance, cadence, concision, rather than to the coarser elements of sense. They are, besides, more plentiful than any but the most determined of correctors would have the patience to make. Such alterations, given their kind and their quantity, are, I submit, of the sort that only an author can be imagined as making. Altogether, they give an unusual opportunity to see Kipling (for I assume that it is Kipling) at work. I have recorded all of the manuscript changes in the 'Textual Variants' in this edition so that any reader who wishes to do so may see the revisions that Kipling made, and form his or her own conclusions as to their principle.

Then there are the new songs – five of them – added to this dramatic version.[11] Without venturing an opinion as to their worth compared with the original songs from the *Jungle Books*, I think it most unlikely that some other hand has done them. The treatment

of the verses taken over from the *Jungle Books* is also highly sugges-
tive: they have been, in almost every instance, slightly and unobtrus-
ively modified to fit their new positions. But these are not arguments,
only points for consideration. The accumulation of external and
internal evidence for Kipling's authorship of *The Jungle Play* seems
to me to put the question beyond doubt; and if there should be
doubters, they will have what I regard as an impossible burden of
disproof to carry.

Kipling and the Theatre

Kipling is not usually thought of in connection with the theatre,
but a close look at his life and work turns up more signs of interest
in the stage than might be suspected. Like most people in an age
that depended largely upon its own efforts for its entertainment,
Kipling knew something about amateur theatricals. There was a
production of Sheridan's *The Rivals* at his school, Westward Ho!,
in which Kipling took the part of Sir Anthony Absolute. In India,
where he lived from 1882 to 1889, he participated in local theatricals
such as a production of *Plot and Passion*, by Tom Taylor and John
Lang, at the Railway Theatre in Lahore. The reviewer in the local
paper noted that Kipling showed in this 'a talent for acting', though
the provincial standard need not have been very high. He appeared
again in a Lahore production of something called *Up a Tree* in
February 1885.[12]

In the course of his journalistic duties in India he had, inevitably,
to attend and to write constructive remarks about all sorts of
theatrical entertainments – burlesque, melodrama, musical – both
amateur and professional. He took a partial revenge for this affliction
by writing a comic sketch about the feckless behaviour of an amateur
dramatics group.[13] When the Rosa Towers company came to Lahore
on tour in 1885, Kipling was assigned to review their performances,
including productions of *Drink* (adapted from Zola's *L'Assommoir*),
Lady Audley's Secret (adapted from Mary Elizabeth Braddon's
sensational novel of that name), and a comic operetta called *Le*

Chalet.[14] Kipling himself was engaged to produce an 'operetta' for the amusement of Simla in the season of 1886; it was evidently written, but something happened to prevent its production.[15] 'The Story of the Gadsbys', a set of stories appearing in the series of 'Railway Library' books that Kipling produced at the end of his Indian years, is written in dramatic form, though Kipling had no thought of seeing it upon the stage.[16]

On his return to England at the end of 1889, Kipling discovered the music hall, then at the peak of its popularity as urban entertainment, and took it very seriously indeed. From his quarters high in a building on Villiers Street, he could, he tells us, look across the road into the depths of Gatti's theatre under the arches of Charing Cross Station. If he crossed the road to the theatre, as he seems to have done regularly, he could, for sixpence, get admission and a pint of porter as well, to be drunk in company with soldiers and servant girls while they were entertained by a Great and Only, a Lion Comique, or 'circular ladies in pale pink and white'. So powerful was the effect of music-hall song upon its audience that Kipling could imagine no higher poetic achievement than to write a successful song in the genre, a conviction that he dramatized in the uncollected story 'My Great and Only'.[17] The power of the music hall is also central to the comic story 'The Village that Voted the Earth Was Flat'. Music-hall entertainment might be vulgar, but it was genuine.

At the same time that he made his discovery of the music hall, Kipling was assiduously studying the legitimate theatre in London: in the first weeks after his arrival in London from India in October 1889, he saw Arthur Wing Pinero's *Sweet Lavender*, Watts Phillips's *The Dead Heart*, Brandon Thomas's *Gold Craze* and Henry Arthur Jones's *The Middleman*.[18] This was a pretty good cross-section of what the English theatre then had on offer: *Sweet Lavender* was a sentimental domestic drama; *The Dead Heart*, a revival from 1859, was a historical drama on the French Revolution; the *Gold Craze* and *The Middleman* were both melodramas of seduction, of aristocratic arrogance, and other staple commodities of the Victorian theatre. Kipling had also made friends with William Ernest Henley, who had collaborated with Robert Louis Stevenson on a series of historical dramas. Soon Kipling was thinking of writing a play himself: he speaks of having one 'on his brain' in August 1890, though we learn nothing further about it.

The turn towards a greater 'seriousness' on the English stage, the turn associated with Ibsen and Shaw, was just about to be made. It is doubtful that Kipling ever saw anything of Shaw's. But he was a friend of Edmund Gosse, who, with William Archer, was the leading sponsor of Ibsen in England, and he went with Gosse to the production of *Hedda Gabler* in April 1891. He noted Ibsen's 'curt and severe' style but beyond that his response is not recorded.[19] It is not likely, though, that Kipling was much impressed by the idea of the stage as an engine of social regeneration. He was, though, interested enough in the theatre to try his hand at adapting *The Light that Failed* for the stage. We know this only from a letter of his agent, A. S. Watt, to the actor-manager Richard Mansfield, who proposed to adapt the novel himself. 'Mr Kipling', Watt wrote in reply to Mansfield in April 1891, 'has for some little time past thought of himself producing a dramatized version of his new novel, and I may say that he has already completed a large portion of the MS of the play.'[20] But no more is heard either from Kipling or Mansfield on this matter, and the manuscript of Kipling's adaptation may probably be added to the list of 'lost' works already mentioned.

Kipling's life in London ended early in 1892 with his marriage and his removal to Vermont, where theatre did not exist. In those years he occasionally notes seeing a play on his excursions to New York or Boston: *Twelfth Night* with Ada Rehan, for example, in New York in 1893. But play-going was hardly a regular activity. Kipling had, by the way, a good knowledge of Shakespeare, as testified to by the wide range of his allusions to the plays. It had been one of the Kipling family's dinner-table amusements in India to cap one another's invented 'quotations' from Shakespeare, an exercise in invention that would not have been possible without a full knowledge. Kipling also enjoyed reading the plays of the English renaissance, and undertook an imitation Elizabethan play called

Gow's Watch, fragments of which appeared as chapter headings in his books between 1901 and 1926. Whether it ever had any completer form is not known.[21] It shows, perhaps, more of Kipling's attraction to parody and imitation than to stage drama. Kipling was also much interested in the Shakespearean essays of his friend Brander Matthews, the American playwright, critic and teacher, especially for their emphasis upon the practical stagecraft of Shakespeare's work.

When, after a four-year interval spent in America, Kipling returned to England in 1896, he settled outside London, so that theatre-going was not a steady but only an intermittent amusement. The hankering to put something on the stage stayed with him, however. After his work on *The Jungle Play* in 1900–1901 he continued to work on ideas for plays, some apparently written, more apparently not. He began one in 1902 called 'The Gods and the Machine', about which nothing further is known. Ten years later, he spent a good deal of time making a play out of his soldier stories, evidently at the request of an American producer.[22] He seems to have been particularly drawn towards writing plays around this time. When his friend Rider Haggard visited Bateman's at the end of September 1911, Kipling read '2 of his plays – and we discussed others, especially one that would deal with the fall of the British Empire'.[23] One play from this period was actually staged – the one-acter *The Harbour Watch*, produced at the Royalty Theatre in 1913; another, the undated one-acter 'Upstairs', survived in manuscript and was published in 1995. The evidence strongly suggests that in his various excursions into playwriting he was not writing closet drama but always aimed at actual stage production. But this takes us beyond the period of *The Jungle Play*.

This rough outline of Kipling's knowledge of the theatre down to the end of the century, when he undertook to dramatize the *Jungle Books*, suggests that he would have had a competent idea of conventional stage practice but nothing more, unless his perception of the seriousness and power of music-hall entertainment be credited as something special. There are, in the stagecraft of *The Jungle Play*, two striking elements that would certainly challenge the skill and imagination of any director. How are the animals to be presented on stage, and how does one manage the music that runs through the play? It is quite possible that the difficulties raised by these things were a part of the reason that *The Jungle Play* never reached the stage despite Kipling's hopes for it.

How did Kipling imagine that we should see the animals of *The Jungle Play*? Were they to be costumed in elaborate imitation of wolves, tigers, jackals, panthers and bears, or was there to be only the lightest of allusions to animal nature? Would the actors disappear into their make-up as animals, or would they retain their individual identities? The stage directions that Kipling has provided do not answer these questions; for the most part they are guides to gesture and tone but not to the spectacular element of costume and setting. And the sorts of gesture indicated, as when Mowgli puts his arm affectionately round Bagheera's neck or Akela sniffs the carcass of Shere Khan, seem to be taken from the narrative of the *Jungle Books* rather than to be adapted to the very different requirements of *The Jungle Play*: it is all very well to read of such actions in a narrative, but how is one to see them on a stage? All this is a reason to suspect that Kipling intended to hand over the manuscript to a theatre professional who would provide the instructions for a stage realization. There is nothing in the play as it stands that would not work in the theatre, one way or another: but what way is indicated?

The songs that are so important a part of the play also raise questions. The combination of story and song is one that Kipling had made particularly his own. Many of his stories are prefaced and concluded by poems that, in different ways, comment or reflect on the stories to which they are attached, sometimes to surprising effect. T. S. Eliot has made the striking suggestion that Kipling arrived at a new form through this method, a form in which story and poems combine to produce a third thing different from the two elements composing it. In any case, the 'songs' (as he called them) attached to Kipling's stories are not merely ornamental. There are also stories, like the *Jungle Books*, that include songs and poems within the text as well as at the beginning and end. Kipling has taken over ten of these for use in *The Jungle Play* and has written five new ones as well.

Some of the songs taken over from the *Jungle Books* for *The Jungle Play* vary slightly from their original forms, suggesting that they have been set down from memory. In the opening scene of the play, for example, the Wolves sing, chorally, the verses that appear as the chapter heading to 'Mowgli's Brothers', the first of the Mowgli stories. In the book, the fifth line runs: 'This is the hour of pride and power'; in the play, it goes: 'This is our hour of pride and power'. Has the change from 'the hour' to 'our hour' occurred as a slip of memory, or as a dramatic touch? In the book, the song is a chapter heading, assigned to no one in particular; in the play, the Wolves sing it, so that there is an obvious reference for the pronoun 'our'. You take your choice.

In other instances, distinct changes have obviously been made in order to adapt the songs to their new places. Thus, after the death of Shere Khan in Act II, Scene 2, we hear 'Chil's Song', originally placed at the end of 'Red Dog' in *The Second Jungle Book* to mark the end of the fight involving scores of wolves and hundreds of dogs. Now it is applied to a single combat between Mowgli and Shere Khan, so the pronouns must change from 'they' to 'he'. More strikingly, in Act IV, Scene 1, we hear the hunting song at the head of 'Red Dog', which, in its original place, ends with a cry celebrating the joy of the hunt: 'It is met, and we go to the fight.' But now it is a different sort of hunt – Dulia, Mowgli's 'Little White One', is about to reappear in his life – and the song takes a surprising turn: 'It is met and we haste to delight!'

The five new songs that Kipling has written for *The Jungle Play*[24] call attention to the fact that the lyric element is even more important in the play than it is in the *Jungle Books*. Indeed, Act IV of *The Jungle Play* is essentially lyric, the slender action being sustained by the songs of Pherao, Dulia and Mowgli. And Kipling has needed new songs to support the love interest of *The Jungle Play*, an interest that the original songs of the *Jungle Books* are hardly calculated to supply.

There are, by my count, some twenty-one musical episodes in

the course of the play, mostly clustered in the first and fourth acts. It is not always clear who sings them, or how distinctly they are to be brought forward as part of the action and meaning of the play rather than being kept to the function of background music. Three of the animals have songs: the Bandar-Log, the Wolves and (off-stage) Pherao the woodpecker. Dulia has three songs, and Mowgli himself two. The rest are assigned simply to 'music', and it would be an important directorial decision to determine how that music is to be managed. I imagine that Kipling meant the words of his songs to be heard quite clearly.[25]

For the rest, *The Jungle Play* is a well-constructed drama, showing a good sense of the effectively theatrical. The speeches are kept brief, the scenes build to clear high points, the process of Mowgli's development holds things together. The two crucial episodes that must be rendered but would be impossible to stage – the pursuit and death of Shere Khan and the destruction of the village – are managed by having Mowgli, on-stage, direct invisible actions off-stage. The audience's expectations in both of these scenes are partly satisfied, at least, by the 'tableau' of Mowgli over the dead Shere Khan in the one, and by the head and shoulders of Hathi looming out of the high grass at the back of the stage in the other.

The *Jungle Books* and *The Jungle Play*

When we speak of *The Jungle Book* we mean, of course, the *Jungle Books*, for there are two of them: *The Jungle Book* of 1894 and *The Second Jungle Book* of 1895. And when we speak of *The Jungle Book* without further qualification, we mean only the Mowgli stories. The two *Jungle Books* together contain fifteen stories, but only eight of them are about Mowgli.[26] The other seven have nothing to do with any jungle and have in common only the fact that they all concern animals in one way or another, including the mongoose Rikki-Tikki-Tavi, the white seal Kotick and the dog Kotuko. Kipling's original working title for the stories that became the *Jungle Books* was 'Noah's Ark Tales',[27] and that perhaps gives a better general notion of their contents than the word 'jungle' does. But it is, of course, the 'jungle' stories proper – that is, the stories about Mowgli – that have captured the imaginations of readers from the moment that they first appeared, and for every one reader who knows about Kotuko the Eskimo dog or Kotik the white seal there must be a thousand who know about Mowgli, Akela and Shere Khan.

The Jungle Play is based on the central four of the eight Mowgli stories – that is, on those stories that trace the development of Mowgli from the moment that he is adopted by the wolf-pack at the Council Rock to the moment when he 'goes back to Man'. The correspondences between the stories in the *Jungle Books* and the parts of *The Jungle Play* are clear: the Prologue and Act I dramatize 'Mowgli's Brothers'; Act II, 'Tiger! Tiger!'; Act III, 'Letting in the Jungle'; Act IV, 'The Spring Running'. Such stories as 'How Fear Came to the Jungle', in which Mowgli is only a listener, or 'Kaa's Hunting' and 'The King's Ankus', in which he is more passive than active, do not figure in *The Jungle Play*. Nor does 'Red Dog', which is all action, but not of a kind that belongs to Kipling's interest in *The Jungle Play*. The Bandar-Log of 'Kaa's Hunting' are too good an invention to be wholly given up, so they are allowed to open the play before they disappear. A couple of songs from 'Red Dog' have also been salvaged for the play, where they appear in contexts much different from those of their original places.

Kipling has adapted the time-scheme a bit in order to meet the need for concentration and unity on the stage. Mowgli is fifteen at the end of Act I, when he is cast out by the wolf-pack; after only three months in the village, he is cast out by the man-pack (Act II). The episode of letting in the Jungle (Act III) follows immediately, and after a year Dulia returns (Act IV) and the play is ended. In the stories, there are indefinite intervals of time between Mowgli's first leaving the Jungle and his return, between his return and the destruction of the village, and after the destruction of the village until the time of the spring running. But, even though the time of action in the play has been shortened, Kipling still imagines the stage Mowgli at the end as of the same, or nearly the same, age as the story Mowgli, who, in 'The Spring Running', is 'nearly seventeen years old'.[28]

At the end of 'Tiger! Tiger!' in its original book form, when Mowgli finds that 'Man–Pack and Wolf-Pack have cast me out' and he therefore becomes a lone hunter, Kipling adds: 'But he was not always alone, because years afterward he became a man and married. But that is a story for grown-ups.'

The Jungle Play is that 'story for grown-ups', developed by the introduction of the character of Dulia and the themes of human love, domesticity and community that her role brings to the action. She has the merest hint of an existence in 'The Spring Running', when Mowgli, stirred by the yearnings of spring, the time of the 'New Talk', encounters, only for a moment, a nameless girl:

Mowgli was going to answer when a girl in a white cloth came down some path that led from the outskirts of the village. Gray Brother dropped out of sight at once, and Mowgli backed noiselessly into a field of high-springing crops. He could almost have touched her with his hand when the warm, green stalks closed before his face and he disappeared like a ghost. The girl screamed, for she thought she had seen a spirit, and then she gave a deep sigh. Mowgli parted the stalks with his hands and watched her till she was out of sight.

This delicately treated moment is revisited and expanded through the character of Dulia, another girl in white. She is an attractive character, modest and dutiful but capable of initiative and, like all of Kipling's women, stronger than the men. And she is utterly assured about her role: to sustain the communal life of humankind in the home and in the village. Dulia's emblem is fire, 'the Red Flower' that 'warms, cherishes and makes clean'. It is from Dulia that Mowgli obtains fire in Act I, and it is Dulia's fire that Mowgli feeds at the end of Act IV: as Mowgli has subdued the hostile animals with fire, so he is himself subdued to it. The song that Dulia sings (in slightly different versions) at the beginning and end of the play puts fire at the centre of human activity:

Ashes of fire at even,
   Smoke to the timeless sky:
And we mourn and we strive,
And we woo and we wive
   But the village endureth for aye.

Gods of the garth and the homestead,
   Gods of the field and the byre;
Grant us the hope of our toiling,
   Love by the light of our fire![29]

At the end of *The Jungle Play*, Mowgli sings, most improbably, a prayer of thanks for the blessing of love and for a state of things 'as it was in Eden'.[30] But we see that, on the whole, the human society exhibited in *The Jungle Play* is anything but Edenic. Since *The Jungle Play* is a story for 'grown-ups', it represents things not only as they might be among loyal animals in a community directed by the Jungle Law but as they are in fact among people. Accordingly, the rather shabby doings of human society are much more prominent in *The Jungle Play* than they are in the *Jungle Books*, especially as seen in the character of Buldeo, who takes on a new prominence in *The Jungle Play*. Lying, greedy, vengeful and incompetent, Buldeo embodies the ignorance and the fears of the village at large. Other things suggest that what Mowgli will find when he leaves the Jungle to return to Man will be difficult. The burden of Dulia's song about human life is constant toil; and that part of 'The Outsong' (as it is called where it originally appeared in *The Second Jungle Book*) that closes the play is about the life of imprisonment that Mowgli must lead after the life of the Jungle – at least that is how the animals see it. The 'new trail' that Mowgli and Dulia will tread leads to a fallen world rather than to the Eden of his song.[31]

It would take a bold critic indeed to say what the *Jungle Books* are 'about'. They show many different faces to different readers, and combine any number of different ways of story-telling. At one extreme they contain 'realistic' elements about Jungle life, points of natural history drawn from such sources as R. A. Sterndale's *Seonee* (1877). At another extreme they touch the purest romance adventure, bordering on the supernatural. The stories are often read as allegories, political or psychological. Mowgli among the animals of the Jungle, for example, has been seen as the image of the English among the Indians, affecting brotherhood but in reality ruling without mercy. And so on. Or the stories are fables; that is to say, not systematic allegories exhibiting point-to-point correspondences between story and subject but illustrating some general truth about life. So Mowgli's instruction in the Law of the Jungle is a fable of the child's initiation into society, a complex process requiring self-denial, respect, obedience and initiative. Or the conflict of Jungle and village illustrates the conflict between the imagination and actuality. Such labellings of the elementary conflicts in the *Jungle Books* no doubt tell us more about the interpreters than they do of the thing ostensibly interpreted. But that is a proof of vitality in the thing itself: it challenges readers to try to pin it down.

It would not be difficult to defend all of these observations, and a great many more that might be made, about the *Jungle Books*. *The Jungle Play* is not so complicated. Most of the romance adventure is gone: the whole situation of the child amidst the talking animals of the Jungle is of course fantastic, but within that fantasy things behave according to reasonable expectation – the wolves behave like wolves, the jackal like a jackal and so on. No magic is exercised, except the magic of Mowgli's power over the Jungle. In *The Jungle Play* there is no episode so strange and wonderful as that of 'Kaa's Hunting' or 'The King's Ankus'. The initiation into the Law of the Jungle, so prominent in the *Jungle Books*, is also missing from *The Jungle Play*, since it is the next phase of his education, his joining the world of human beings, that occupies Mowgli now.

In more than one way the nearest thing to *The Jungle Play* in Kipling's work is *Kim*. Kipling was finishing *Kim* at the end of 1900, and he appears to have taken up work on *The Jungle Play* immediately after *Kim* was off his hands, so that the one succeeds the other in the calendar of Kipling's work.[32] Both *Kim* and *The Jungle Play* have 'amphibious' heroes: Mowgli ('the Frog'), moving between the worlds of animals and of people; Kim, even more supple and adaptable, moving between native and European, childish and adult, material and spiritual worlds. And for both Mowgli and Kim, the critical question is to determine where each belongs. Again, the question seems simpler for Mowgli: no one doubts that he is 'man', and 'man goes to man at the last'. The emphasis of this conclusion is rather different than in the *Jungle Books*, where many readers have seen Mowgli as neither of the Jungle nor of the village but apart from and above them both. Incidentally, Mowgli's choice of a wife and the life of the village in *The Jungle Play* makes nonsense of the view that he is the embodiment of the British imperial idea. But then that may be another way in which the play differs from the stories.

It is not so clear where Kim belongs, or whether he can answer his own question, 'What is Kim?' But both Mowgli and Kim imagine that in some way they have succeeded in uniting, in their own experience, the different and conflicting worlds that they have known: 'There is one law for ye, and another for me,' as Mowgli tells the animals in his farewell, 'but the love between us shall bind us as strongly as that law.'[33]

EDITORIAL NOTE

In transcribing Kipling's typescript, I have silently corrected what seemed to me to be simple typographical errors ('fried' for 'friend', 'Messura' for 'Messua', 'excaped' for 'escaped'). In addition, I have frequently altered the punctuation and capitalization but without fully regularizing them.

Places at which alterations in the text have been made in Kipling's hand are indicated by a superscript number. The changes so indicated are set forth, act by act, in the 'Textual Variants' at the end of *The Jungle Play*.

NOTES

1 In the summary of Caroline Kipling's now-destroyed diary made by Douglas Rees for the use of Lord Birkenhead when Birkenhead was writing his life of Kipling. A copy is at the University of Sussex.

2 Thomas Pinney (ed.), *The Letters of Rudyard Kipling*, III (Macmillan, London, 1996), 38: 2 December 1900.

3 *Letters*, III, 64. For much of the time between beginning *The Jungle Play* at the end of 1900 and revising it in June 1901, Kipling had been on his annual visit to South Africa (20 January–11 April 1901). There is no evidence that he worked on the play in that interval, though there is no reason why he should not have done.

4 The first recorded suggestion for dramatizing *The Jungle Book* was that it be put on as a Christmas pantomime. Kipling discusses the idea in an undated letter, probably from late 1895:

The notion has been much thought upon and a lot of men this side and the other suggested it for a regular Xmas pantomime. But – there is only one Lauri, he who does dogs and things at Drury Lane so that you weep at the Beasts's emotions: and to carry the notion through so that it wouldn't be shrieking farce would need a dozen of him. Some one suggested too that Hagermann's beasts should be trained to do scenes. I'd love to see it but I fear it's hopeless.

(Letter to William Carey: Huntington Library, California.)

Henry ('Harry') Lauri (Albert Henry Lowe) was one of a family of panto-mime clowns; he died in 1886, but Kipling may not have known that. 'Hagermann' may be a stab at 'Hagenbeck', the famous Hamburg menagerie.

5 *Letters*, III, 38: 2 December 1900.

6 This bears the signature of the distinguished American director Frank Capra on the cover. Capra had made his entry into film-making with a twelve-minute version of Kipling's 'The Ballad of Fisher's Boarding-House'. No film version of 'The Gate of the Hundred Sorrows' has been made, though a scenario that Kipling made in collaboration with Randolph Lewis was published in the *New York Times* (29 April 1923).

7 This script was in fact by Kipling, or rather was the result of a collaboration with A. R. Rawlinson, and contains a good many corrections by Kipling. It bears no resemblance to the film eventually released in 1939 as *Gunga Din*.

8 It is box 25, file 11, of the Kipling Papers at Sussex.

9 Kipling had had a secretary since 1899; one of her main jobs was to type all of his manuscripts before they were sent out to his agent. The rule, strictly enforced, was that nothing in his own handwriting was sent out for publication. The first secretary, who remained with him through 1901 and who must therefore have typed the extant copy of *The Jungle Play*, was Sara Anderson, who had also worked for Ruskin, Meredith and George Moore. While she was in Kipling's employ (he was then living in Rotting-dean), she also assisted Lady Burne-Jones with her *Memorials of Burne-Jones*.

10 This leads me to the Higher Editing. Take of well-ground Indian Ink as much as suffices and a camel-hair brush proportionate to the inter-spaces of your lines. In an auspicious hour, read your final draft and consider faithfully every paragraph, sentence and word, blacking out where requisite. Let it lie by to drain as long as possible. At the end of that time, re-read and you should find that it will bear a second shortening. Finally, read it aloud alone and at leisure. Maybe a shade more brushwork will then indicate or impose itself.

(*Something of Myself*, Macmillan, London, 1937, pp. 207–8.)

If Kipling followed this prescription strictly, then the typescript of *The Jungle Play* must represent a very late stage of revision.

11 These are: 'Ashes of fire at even' (Act I, Scene 2; again in Act IV, Scene 1); 'Now I was born of woman kind' (Act III, Scene 1); two separate stanzas of 'Pherao's Song' (Act IV, Scene 1): 'With the faithful sun and the fruitful cloud' and 'She has stirred the sap of the oldest tree'; 'My Lord is lord of the Lord of the Night' (Act IV, Scene 1); 'He that soweth the streams in the sea' (Act IV, Scene 1).

12 He was also to have appeared in local productions of W. S. Gilbert's *Palace of Truth* and in Maddison Morton's farce *Woodcock's Little Game* in 1884 but was prevented by 'a very sudden indisposition' (*Civil and Military Gazette*, 16 April 1884).

13 'Le Monde où l'On S'Amuse' (*Civil and Military Gazette*, 1 October 1887: uncollected).

14 Other reviews that Kipling wrote include one of an American melo-drama, *Young Mrs Winthrop*, put on by an amateur company in Simla (*Civil and Military Gazette*, 23 June 1885: uncollected).

15 I have to report that I am under contract to write a Comic Operetta on an Anglo Indian subject for Simla this season. I've got it all out in the rough and it only needs pulling together – a longer business than one expects. It's very very Anglo Indian and I don't think it would be intelligible at home. However my fellow worker – the man who is setting the music – says it's pretty certain to take here. Anything amuses a land of people who are always at work.

(*Letters*, I, 121:18–27 February 1886.)

Kipling's verse during his Indian years frequently takes the form of Gilbert and Sullivan imitations; that model would no doubt have had a good deal of effect on any operetta he might imagine.

16 It was, however, produced as a play in New York with some success in 1980.

17 *Civil and Military Gazette*, 11 and 15 January 1890.

18 See Roger Lancelyn Green's identification of the plays alluded to at the beginning of 'My Great and Only' (in R. E. Harbord (ed.), *The Reader's Guide to Rudyard Kipling's Works*, II, privately printed, 1963, 707–8). Kipling arrived in London in the first week of October 1889; 'My Great and Only' was written on 16 November (*Letters*, I, 366).

19 *Letters*, II, 34.

20 A. S. Watt to Richard Mansfield, 16 April 1891 (Berg Collection, New York Public Library).

21 The fragments are partly collected in the volume called *Rudyard Kipling's Verse: Definitive Edition* (Hodder & Stoughton, London, 1940, pp. 617–27), where they are said to be 'enlarged from various sources'.

22 This had been suggested as long ago as 1901, when Mrs Kipling noted that they had received a proposal from the American publisher S. S. McClure 'for a big American theatrical trust to dramatise "Soldiers Three" ' (Mrs Kipling's diary in the Rees extracts: 9 September 1901).

23 Morton Cohen (ed.), *Rudyard Kipling to Rider Haggard* (Hutchinson, London, 1965), p. 69.

24 See note 11.

25 There would be no difficulty in finding settings for the original songs from the *Jungle Books*, which have attracted several composers. Percy Grainger composed a *Jungle Book Cycle* of eleven settings; other composers who have published *Jungle Book* settings include Cyril Scott, Robert Atkinson, Dora Bright, Homer Hatch and Maurice Delage.

26 They are, from *The Jungle Book*, 'Mowgli's Brothers', 'Kaa's Hunting' and 'Tiger! Tiger!'; from *The Second Jungle Book*, 'How Fear Came', 'Letting in the Jungle', 'The King's Ankus', 'Red Dog' and 'The Spring Running'. There is another Mowgli story, 'In the Rukh', published before the *Jungle Books* in *Many Inventions* (1893). I agree with Daniel Karlin and others in regarding 'In the Rukh' as the product of a wholly separate inspiration, forming no part of the *Jungle Books* (see Karlin, introduction to *The Jungle Books*, Penguin Books, London, 1987, pp. 12–13 and note).

27 *Letters*, II, 72: 24 November [1892].

28 In Act IV, Baloo says that Mowgli has heard the woodpecker's spring song 'seventeen times since thou wast a cub': since Mowgli is described as a 'three year old naked baby' in Act I, Mowgli would be twenty at the end of the play. I prefer to think that here Kipling has made a slip in writing 'seventeen times': he is thinking of Mowgli's age rather than of the years elapsed in the Jungle.

29 This is the text in Act IV; it varies from that in Act I, Scene 2, which ends:

> Grant us the fruit of our toiling
> Peace by the light of our fire!

30 How is it that Mowgli, whose ignorance of theology is such that he must ask, 'What is a devil?' (Act III, Scene 2), can now allude easily to 'Eden' and the 'four great rivers'? By direct inspiration?

31 In 'The Outsong' stanza as sung at the end of the play, Kipling has omitted these three lines that appear in the book:

> In the dawns when thou shalt wake
> To the toil thou canst not break,
> Heartsick for the Jungle's sake:

Perhaps he thought this too discordant a note to be sounded at the moment of Mowgli and Dulia's joy in each other; it also confuses the decision in favour of the human community over the Jungle.

32 Kipling sent off the last proofs of *Kim* on 9 September 1900; on 15 November he is first reported as working on *The Jungle Play* (Mrs Kipling's diary in the Rees extracts).

33 There is nothing quite equivalent to this in the scene of Mowgli's farewell in 'The Spring Running'.

Note to the Penguin Edition

Since the original edition of this book, new information has been found about its history. A contract between Kipling and the actor and producer Henry H. H. Cameron, dated 4 December 1900, is in the A. P. Watt Papers now at the University of North Carolina, Chapel Hill. The contract gives Cameron the right to produce the play on or before 31 December 1901 at the Lyceum or 'some other first-class West End Theatre in London with an appropriate musical setting . . . The Manager [Cameron] shall at his own costs produce suitable and appropriate music to be composed for the production and representation of the said play and shall make all arrangements as to the supply of such music.' On his part, Kipling undertook to deliver a finished script on or before 21 May 1901. What happened to prevent the production of the play remains unknown, but the contract shows that Kipling intended to see his play staged.

Illustrations

A NOTE ON THE ILLUSTRATIONS

The pen and ink sketches of scenes from *The Jungle Book* reproduced here were made by Kipling in order to assist W. H. Drake, who illustrated the two Mowgli stories ('Mowgli's Brothers' and 'Tiger! Tiger!') published in the American magazine *Saint Nicholas* in January and February 1894. The drawings were thus probably made late in 1893. They were preserved by Samuel Chapin, then on the staff of *Saint Nicholas*. In an undated note accompanying the drawings in the Amherst College Library, Chapin gave this account of their history:

These crude sketches were made by Rudyard Kipling at the time of the first publication of his Jungle Stories in the St Nicholas Magazine, as guides to the artist who illustrated the stories. Mr Kipling was very particular that details of clothing, furniture, etc., should be quite correct; hence these rough sketches, which, although not signed, are unquestionably the work of his own hand. In the course of the publication of the Jungle Stories they finally drifted to an anchorage on my desk from which the 'make-up' of each issue got its start.

These drawings are now reproduced, for the first time, by the courtesy of the Amherst College Library, Chapin-Kiley Collection, Archives and Special Collections.

1. *The wolf cave*

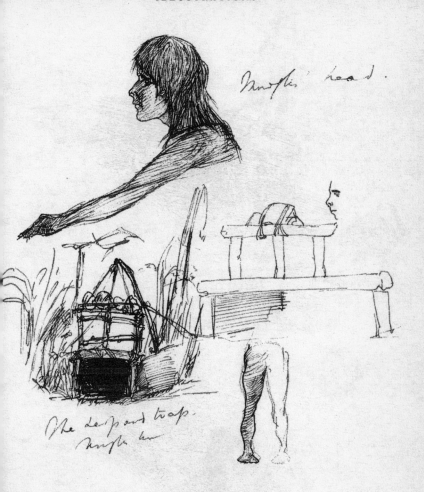

2. *Mowgli and a jungle trap*

3. *Mowgli in the village and on the Council Rock*

4. *Baloo and Bagheera*

5. *Bagheera, Mowgli, Buffalo*

6. *Village, grazing ground, Jungle*

7. *Village club and herd-bull*

8. *The herd at dusk*

9. *Children's games*

THE JUNGLE PLAY

DRAMATIS PERSONÆ

Mowgli, the Frog, the Man-Cub
Bandar-Log, the Monkey People
Baloo, the Bear
Bagheera, the Black Panther
Akela, the Lone Wolf, leader of the Wolf-Pack
Mother Wolf, Raksha the Demon
Tabaqui, the Jackal
Shere Khan, the Lame Tiger
Grey Brother, a Wolf
Dulia, the daughter of Messua and Rawal
Rawal, a prosperous farmer
Messua, wife of Rawal
Buldeo, the Village Hunter
First Villager
Second Villager
Third Villager
Priest
Hathi, the Elephant
Pherao, the Woodpecker
Nameless Wolves, Villagers

PROLOGUE

THE COUNCIL ROCK

Here we go in a flung festoon,
Half way up to the jealous moon!
Don't you envy our pranceful bands?
Don't you wish you had extra hands?
Wouldn't you like if your tails were – *so* –
Curved in the shape of a Cupid's Bow?
> Now, you're angry, but never mind.
> *Brother, thy tail hangs down behind!**

'Road-Song of the Bandar-Log' as AKELA *appears on the top of the Council Rock, and the* WOLVES *group themselves.* BALOO *and* BAGHEERA *are couched in long grass to the right. The* MONKEYS *are seated on broken rocks to the left, and in trees above.*

THE BANDAR-LOG [*confusedly*]: Good hunting, Free People! They think themselves too fine to notice us.[1] Throw rubbish at them.[2] *We* are the people of the Jungle. Hi! Hi!
AKELA: To the Rock! To the Council Rock! To the Council! It is met!
WOLVES:

> Now Rann the Kite brings home the night
> That Mang the Bat sets free –

* The first stanza of 'Road-Song of the *Bandar-Log*', at the end of 'Kaa's Hunting' (*The Jungle Book*).

3

> The herds are shut in byre and hut
>> For loosed till dawn are we.
> This is our hour of pride and power,
>> Talon and tooth and claw.
> Then hear the call! – Good hunting all
>> That keep the Jungle Law!*

A MONKEY: Let me see! What do the Free People?[3]

A MONKEY: Look over their dirty cubs. Good hunting, Free People![4] [*Shakes branch.*]

AKELA: Look well, O Wolves! Ye know the Law! These are the new cubs of the year to be entered to the pack. Look and accept.[5] Here is White-Tooth's cub! Here is Lahini's cub! Look well, O Wolves! Here is Black-Tail's cub!** – Does a Wolf[6] dispute their right to run with the pack?

[WOLVES *move forward under the Council Rock, advancing and retiring rhythmically as they inspect cubs.*]

WOLVES: We have seen. We accept.[7] They shall be wolves of the pack. – Free Hunters under the moon.

AKELA: Here are Mother Wolf's cubs – and here is a man-cub† fostered by Mother Wolf. A man-cub, the son of a man. Look well, O Wolves!

[*A small three-year-old naked baby staggers across, and sits down in moonlight under the rock.*]

A MONKEY: Ah! Now the nuts will fall! What is the creature[8] doing here, Tabaqui? [*Stoops to pull* TABAQUI's *tail.*]

TABAQUI [*right*]: It will not stay very long,[9] most honourable Bandar-

---

* 'Night-Song in the Jungle', chapter heading to 'Mowgli's Brothers' (*The Jungle Book*). In the first English edition and in *Rudyard Kipling's Verse: Definitive Edition* (Hodder & Stoughton, London, 1940), it is 'Chil' not 'Rann'. 'Rann' is in the first American edition and the English trade edition. There are two variants in *The Jungle Play* text of the poem: 'our hour' for 'the hour' (line 5); and 'tooth' for 'tush' (line 6).
** None of these names appears in the *Jungle Books*. 'Lahini' is used in 'Red Dog' (*The Second Jungle Book*) for 'she-wolf'. In his 'Author's Notes on the Names in the *Jungle Books*' (Sussex Edition), Kipling says that 'Lahini' is 'a made-up name'.
† In the *Jungle Books*, the term is always 'man's cub'; in *The Jungle Play*, it is always 'man-cub'.

4

Log. It belongs to my master, Shere Khan, the Lame Tiger. He tracked it up to Mother Wolf's cave a month ago; but it was thin and poor, so he gave[10] Mother Wolf orders to feed it until it grew fat. He kills it to-night[11] and – I am promised the ankle bones.

[*All this while the* WOLVES *are coming forward and retiring as they look over the cubs.*]

A MONKEY: Bravo Tabaqui! You ought to be one of us. You tell a tale so prettily. Most honourable Bandar-Log, hear what really happened. Shere Khan was hunting man. He came on[12] the trail of a man-child lost in the Jungle – a little cub who could hardly walk. Shere Khan is very brave; he followed[13] that trail up to Mother Wolf's lair.

AKELA: Look well, O Wolves! the cubs of the Mother Wolf and – a man-cub.

[*The* WOLVES *are ranged in a suspicious semi-circle round the baby.*]

MONKEY: The man-child strayed into Mother Wolf's cave and Mother Wolf took a fancy to it.[14] She told Shere Khan to come inside and fight for the kill if he dared![15] But he was afraid! He went away growling. Ho! Ho! All the Jungle knows that[16] Shere Khan is as big a cur as Tabaqui.

TABAQUI: See what one gets from trying to be friendly with one's inferior. You will hear my master speak in a moment, then you will be afraid.

MONKEYS: And your master will hear Mother Wolf speak in a moment: and then he'll be afraid – again. Are they going to accept the man-cub, or will they eat him?

AKELA: Look well, O Wolves.

A WOLF: Akela, Lone Wolf – Whose is this naked man-cub –

MOTHER WOLF: Mine by Lair-right. It came to me, naked, alone and fearless. Therefore I spared it – I, Raksha the Demon. My milk is in its blood. Accept it, Wolves.[17]

SHERE KHAN [*left*]: The cub is mine! Give him to me. What have the Free People to do with a man-cub?

AKELA: What have the Free People to do with orders from any except the Free People? Look well, O Wolves!

WOLVES: Accept him! No! He is a man-cub! Cast him out. Let him die.[18] What have the Free People to do with a man-cub? Kill him! Kill.

MOTHER WOLF [*coming forward*]: Then ye kill me, for he is my foster-child. There is my milk in his blood! Who fights Raksha the Demon? Who? [*Child runs to* MOTHER WOLF.]

AKELA: Hold! Ye know the Law. If there is any dispute as to the right of a cub to be entered into the pack, the cub must be spoken for by two of the Jungle-people, who are not his father or his mother.

SHERE KHAN: I am his father and his mother. I ate them both. [*The* MONKEYS *laugh*.] Give him to me. He escaped me once.

AKELA: Quiet, striped cattle-killer![19] Who speaks for this man-cub, the foster-child of Mother Wolf? Among the Free People, who speaks?

MOTHER WOLF [*crouching*]: I may not speak for him, but I will[20] die for him.

AKELA: Do[21] none of the pack speak for him? Then by the Jungle Law[22] I may ask Baloo who teaches our cubs the Jungle Law. He is old: he is wise. Baloo, wilt thou speak for the man-cub?

BALOO [*rising clumsily, bear fashion*]: The man-cub! The man-cub! There is no harm in a man's cub. Yes. *I* will speak for the man-cub. Let him run with the pack. When he is old enough, I myself will teach him the Law!

MOTHER WOLF: Long life, and the best of bees' nests for thee, oh Baloo.

BALOO: It is nothing! it is nothing. I eat honey and roots. I do not love flesh eating[23] – I –

AKELA: Baloo has spoken for the man-cub; we need[24] yet another. Who speaks beside Baloo?

SHERE KHAN: What is this talk of man-cubs accepted by the Free Hunters?[25] He is *my* meat: give him to me. Why does all the Jungle befriend this naked thing?[26]

BAGHEERA [*raising head snakily and insinuatingly*]: O Akela, and ye the Free People! I am not all the Jungle, but only Bagheera, of whom ye may have heard. May I speak?

MONKEYS: Listen – listen to Bagheera. Soft and quiet as a snake! But we know him – we know him.[27]

AKELA: Bagheera[28] is a Lord of Life and Death* in the Jungle. Let him speak.

BAGHEERA [*voice always very sweet and oily*]: The Law of the Jungle says that the life of a cub in the wolf-pack may be bought at a price. But the Law does *not* say who may, or who may not, pay that price.

WOLVES [*falling back from baby, and devoting more attention to* BAGHEERA]: Good! The cub can be bought for a price. It is the Law! Listen to Bagheera.

BAGHEERA: To kill a naked cub is shame.[29] Besides he may make better sport for ye when he is bigger. Baloo has spoken for him. Now to Baloo's word, I will give a young bull that I have killed not half a mile from here. The meat of a fat bull, for the life of a lean man-cub. Choose!

WOLVES [*confusedly*]: Accept! Refuse! What matter? He will die in the rains. He will scorch in the sun! What harm can such a cub do to us? We do not get full[30] gorge every night. Take the bull![31] The bull!

AKELA: Look well, O Wolves!

BAGHEERA: Do ye take my price, Free Hunters?

WOLVES: We take the price. We will accept the man-cub to run with us in the pack, as a free hunter under the moon . . . Let us[32] get to our gorge! The bull! The bull!

MONKEYS: And the Free People call us greedy![33] Come brothers! and mock them while they eat their bull.[34]

[*Exeunt* WOLVES, *all except* MOTHER WOLF *and* AKELA.]

BALOO: That was well done.[35] I do not love killing – I.

SHERE KHAN [*to* BAGHEERA]: Good hunting, Black Cat of the Jungle. Thou hast cheated me of my meat.

BAGHEERA: Thy meat, Painted Butcher of man. Then why didst thou not kill the thing when ye first found it?[36]

---

* This title, which recurs throughout the play, is not in the *Jungle Books*. In 'The Finest Story in the World' (*Many Inventions*, 1893), the 'Lords of Life and Death' are repeatedly invoked, but there they have a very different meaning as the powers who control the memory of the past. (I owe this reference to Mrs Lisa Lewis.)

TABAQUI: My noble master had grievously lamed his foot.

MOTHER WOLF: I gave him leave if he would first kill me. *I* was ready for the fight. He knows it. He was afraid.

SHERE KHAN: Come away, Tabaqui. Those who bathe in dirty water must expect a soiled coat.[37] Another time I will kill first and talk later. Let the man–cub and his pack look to it.[38]

[*Exit* SHERE KHAN *and* TABAQUI.]

BALOO: Very well matched[39] – a lame tiger and a lying jackal.

BAGHEERA: Let them go. If I know anything of man this naked cub will some day make Shere Khan to roar another tune. Men are very wise – eh, Akela?

AKELA: Very wise. They have even trapped me, in my time – and I am the Head Wolf of the pack.

BAGHEERA: Think of the days when thou art old – when thou canst no longer lead the pack or kill buck. Then the pack will turn against thee and kill thee. It is the Law, Head Wolf.

AKELA: I am the Head Wolf. I know what the end of the Head Wolf must be. I have seen many Head Wolves die fighting by the Council Rock.

BAGHEERA: When that day comes, may be thou wilt be glad of the help of a man–cub, who knows both the cunning of wolves and the cunning of men. He may even help thee out of some trap.

AKELA: Was I littered yesterday? I could have slain the man–cub with one blow of my paw if I had chosen. But why didst thou speak for the man–cub, Bagheera; a kill more or less is nothing to thee.

BAGHEERA: I am a Lord of Life and Death in the Jungle. At my pleasure I kill; at my pleasure I let my prey go. It pleased me to spare the man–cub.

MOTHER WOLF [*nosing baby*]: He shall live – he shall live to be a great hunter. Maybe he shall live to slay Shere Khan.

AKELA: Take him away, Mother Wolf, and train him as befits one of the Free People. Look! The day breaks! Good rest!

[*Exeunt.*]

Song

One moment past our bodies cast
    No shadow on the plain;
Now clear and black they stride our track,
    And we run home again.
In morning-hush, each rock and bush
    Stands hard, and high, and raw:
Then give the Call: *'Good rest to all*
    *That keep the Jungle Law!'**

* 'Morning Song in the Jungle', from 'Letting in the Jungle' (*The Second Jungle Book*).

ACT I

SCENE I

The Jungle – as Dawn is breaking. Enter MOWGLI *considering
the ground.*

MOWGLI: Huh! So the pack are out already and before sunset. Why
did they not send me word[1] ... Here went Akela – here went
the others, hunting close. [*Kneeling.*] Hai! That is Grey Brother's
track, and he is running lame. Another thorn in his foot for
Mowgli to pull out[2] with his man-paws[3] ... I will pull Grey
Brother's whiskers too for not telling me of the hunt.[4] Shall I
follow the trail? Yes. [*Yawns.*] No! ... I am all sleepy still ...
But they should have told me ... The Jungle is very still this
day. Ah! Who is afoot? Oh! Good hunting, Grey Brother![5]

GREY BROTHER: Good hunting, Little Brother. I have come back
to thee, because –[6]

MOWGLI [*laughing*]: Because of a thorn in thy foot, I know it ...
Up with thy paw, old grey muzzle. [*Pulls it out.*] Where do we
hunt to-night?

GREY BROTHER [*uneasily*]: In the valley – a strong buck. But there
is no need for thee to come.

MOWGLI: Mowgli will say what Mowgli needs or does not need.

GREY BROTHER: But the Lame Tiger is afoot and – and –

MOWGLI: Shere Khan? What is he to me more than any other
painted cat with a bad breath?

GREY BROTHER: May be, but – ... Stay here awhile with Bagheera and those that love thee; do not hunt[7] with us to-night. [*Exit* GREY BROTHER.]

MOWGLI: But – but – hold the trail an instant . . . I *will* come.

[*Music (off): 'As the dawn was breaking the wolf-pack yelled'.*]*

The red mange eat up their hides for this. I have hunted with my pack since I could kill for myself. I sit at Akela's right foot on the Council Rock, and forsooth I must not hunt with them to-night. By the Bull that bought me, by the Bull Bagheera paid for me, why must I not** hunt with them?

[*Music: 'Ere Mao the peacock flutters', etc.*]†

TABAQUI [*head peering out of the thicket*]: I know – ha! ha! Lord of all the Jungle – most honourable little ape – I know!

MOWGLI: O, dishlicker of Shere Khan, hast thou crossed the ranges with thy thief of a master?

TABAQUI: By the favour of the Great Lord of the Jungle, I have ventured to do so. I am but a jackal – yet *I* can hunt where I choose.

MOWGLI: Yes – sick chickens[8] outside the village gates! Be off with thy hunting!

TABAQUI: I eat when my master has killed. He follows big game to-night, and he has promised me the ankle-bones. Little white bones under the Council Rock, when the moon rises, ha! ha!

MOWGLI: The Lame Tiger kill at the Council Rock. He dare not! That is *our* ground.

TABAQUI: But he will – he will.

MOWGLI [*leaping towards the thicket*]: Am I the man-cub, or am I the mock of the Jungle?

TABAQUI [*withdrawing*]: The mock of the Jungle! Oh ho! The mock

---

* First line, third stanza, of 'Hunting-Song of the Seeonee Pack', at the end of 'Mowgli's Brothers' (*The Jungle Book*).

** The typescript reads 'now'.

† First line of 'The Song of the Little Hunter', at the end of 'The King's Ankus' (*The Second Jungle Book*). In the English edition of *The Second Jungle Book* and in the *Definitive Edition*, the peacock is called 'Mor'; in the American edition, it is 'Mao'. According to R. E. Harbord, *The Readers' Guide to Rudyard Kipling's Works*, VII (privately printed, 1972), 2958, 'Mao' is the 'native name for the peacock'.

of the Jungle. Good hunting . . . little ankle-bones. We shall be friends[9] at the Council Rock.

MOWGLI [*checking himself and scornfully*]: Bah! Tabaqui and the Monkey People are like an old trail – not worth following. But I will follow the pack-trail into the valley; and I will hunt with my pack to-night, and at the Council Rock I will ask them why they did not tell me.

[*Enter* BAGHEERA.]

BAGHEERA: Good hunting, Little Brother! Stay awhile. What is the haste? Hast thou killed?

MOWGLI: Not to-night. I go with the pack now.

BAGHEERA: Softly on that trail. An empty belly is better than an opened[10] throat. *I* know thy wolves.

MOWGLI: By the Bull that bought me, ye all tread one track. First comes Grey Brother with a thorn in his foot saying: 'Do not hunt with the pack.' Next comes Tabaqui with a thorn under his tongue, talking some foolish talk or other. Then comes Bagheera – *my* Bagheera –

BAGHEERA: Who loves thee. Sit down at my side. Yes, and Bagheera says also to his manling: – 'Do not hunt with the pack to-night.'

MOWGLI: Why? I am a Free Hunter under the moon, with the rest.

BAGHEERA: Oh man-cub, man-cub. Hast thou lived so long with us not to know when there is fear in the Jungle? Hark!

[*Music: 'When the moon has cleared the rock ridge'.*]*

MOWGLI: I heard a nut drop and a branch crack.

[*Music: 'On thy knees and draw the bow'.*]**

[*Listening.*] Something is afoot – What? What moves in the Jungle?

BAGHEERA: Fear!

MOWGLI: I have never seen it. [*Sinking at* BAGHEERA*'s side.*] Is this a new thing in the Jungle?

BAGHEERA: The oldest of all . . . [*Growling.*] How oft have I told thee Shere Khan is thy enemy?

---

* Presumably a recollection of the first line of the second stanza of 'The Song of the Little Hunter': 'Ere the moon has climbed the mountain . . .'
** 'The Song of the Little Hunter', stanza 2, line 5.

MOWGLI: As many times as there are nuts in a palm. What of it?[11]

BAGHEERA: What of it? Baloo knows: I know: the pack knows: even the deer know. Did not Tabaqui tell thee?

MOWGLI: Tabaqui came to me just now with some silly tale about my white ankle-bones. I chased[12] him away.

BAGHEERA: That was foolish. Listen to me, Little Brother. Shere Khan has not all these years dared to kill thee in the Jungle for fear of those that love thee; but remember, Akela, the Head Wolf, is old,[13] and soon the day comes when he cannot kill his buck. Then[14] he will lead the pack no more. Many of the wolves that looked thee over when thou wast brought to the Council first are old too, and the young wolves believe, as Shere Khan has taught them, that a man-cub has no place with the pack. In a little time thou wilt be a man.

MOWGLI: And what is a man that he should not run with his brothers? Surely the wolves are my brothers?

BAGHEERA: Little Brother, feel under my jaw. [MOWGLI *puts hand up*.] There is no one in the Jungle knows that I, Bagheera, carry that mark – the mark of the collar – the great iron collar, and yet, Little Brother, I was born among men – in the cages of a king's palace was I born. It was for *this* that I paid the price for thee at the Council when thou wast a little naked cub. I too was born among men as thou wast born. Men fed me behind iron bars till, one night, I felt that I was Bagheera, the Panther, and no man's plaything, and I broke the silly lock with one blow of my paw and came away; and because I had learned the ways of men, I became more terrible in the Jungle than Shere Khan. Is it not so?

MOWGLI: Yes, all the Jungle fears Bagheera – all except Mowgli.

BAGHEERA: Oh, *thou* art a man's cub, and even as I returned to my Jungle, so thou must go back to men at last – if thou art not killed by thy pack.

MOWGLI: What have I to do with men? Why should my brothers kill me?

BAGHEERA: Look at me. [MOWGLI *puts arm round* BAGHEERA*'s neck.* BAGHEERA *turns head aside.*]

MOWGLI: Nay – look at *me*! Why dost thou blink?

BAGHEERA: *That* is why. Not even I can look thee between the eyes, and I was born among men, and I love thee, Little Brother. The others, they hate thee because their eyes cannot meet thine; because thou art wise; because thou hast pulled out thorns from their feet – because thou art a man – a man.

MOWGLI: I did not know these things. [*Scowls.*] It is a bad trail.

BAGHEERA: What is the Law of the Jungle? Strike first and then give tongue. But be wise. It is in my heart that when Akela misses his next kill – and they hunt a very strong buck to-night – the pack will turn against him and against thee. They will hold a Council at the Rock, and the wolves who follow Shere Khan will slay thee.

MOWGLI: Then I die. That is a little thing but – but I loved my brother. *That*[15] hurts me like a sharp thorn.

BAGHEERA [*after a pause*]: Thou[16] shalt not die. Was I born among men for nothing? Go down quickly to the men's huts in the valley, and bring back some of the Red Flower which they grow there, so that when the need comes thou mayst have a strong friend at the Council Rock. Get the Red Flower.

MOWGLI: What do I need of it?[17] *Thou*[18] art my friend, Black Cat.

BAGHEERA: The Red Flower is stronger than us all. When we smell it we crouch like Jungle-fowl. When we see it we grow mad with fear. I – even I – fear it, though I was born among men. Get the Red Flower.

MOWGLI: The Red Flower! It grows outside men's huts in the twilight, and dances inside them after dark.[19] What is there to fear in the Red Flower? I will get some.

BAGHEERA: There speaks the man-cub. Get it swiftly, and bring it to the Rock to-night.

MOWGLI: I go, and my Lair-Mother shall come with me. But art thou sure [*kneels, arm round* BAGHEERA*'s neck*], O my Bagheera, that this is Shere Khan's doing?

BAGHEERA: By the Broken Lock that freed me, I am sure, Little Brother.

MOWGLI: Then, by the Bull that bought me, I will pay Shere Khan full gorge[20] for this, and it may be a little over. [*Rises to go out. Enter* MOTHER WOLF.]

MOTHER WOLF: I came to warn thee, my son! Hunt with me alone, to-night.

MOWGLI: I am warned already, Mother. Hunt with me alone to-night – near the village – and I can hear thy tale on the road. [*Exit.*]

BAGHEERA: That is a man. That is all a man. The Rock to-night, when the moon rises. [*Aside.*] I am a Lord of Life and Death in the Jungle but I would [not] be in thy hide to-night, Shere Khan.[21]

SCENE 2

Outside MESSUA*'s hut in the twilight.* DULIA *lighting a fire of small sticks.*

DULIA [*sings*]:

> Ashes of fire at even
>> Smoke to the timeless sky,
> And we mourn and we strive and we woo and we wive,
>> But the village endureth for aye.
>
> Gods of the garth[22] and the homestead –
>> Gods of the field and the byre
> Grant us the fruit of our toiling
>> Peace by the light of our fire!

and now it is alight. [*Calls to hut.*] Mother, has my father eaten?

RAWAL: Excellently – excellently. Where is my pipe, Dulia?

MESSUA [*standing in the doorway, proudly*]: She made the curry herself, Rawal.

RAWAL [*tenderly*]: Daughters and bamboos grow up in a night . . . She will be a woman soon. Well – well, she shall have her dowry when her time comes to cook for a husband, and, speaking of families, Messua, the dun cow calved last night. It is not so bad. Our herds grow – our herds grow. [*Puffs prosperously.*]

MESSUA: The Gods avert the evil eye, my husband. We plough too near the Jungle to boast of our cattle.

DULIA: I wish our fences grew too, Mother. The wild pig have broken into the millet again.[23]

RAWAL [*smoking*]: Wait till I have finished my ploughing and I'll mend them.[24]

MESSUA: But the pigs won't wait – nor the deer for that matter . . . and the way the monkeys steal half our fruit[25] . . . I can't be housewife and scarecrow both.

RAWAL: That is the price we pay for our rich soil.

MESSUA: Price, indeed!! We have to fight[26] the beasts for every mouthful we eat . . . Ah, if only my son Nathoo had lived.

RAWAL: What is done is done: but we certainly need another pair of hands on the homestead.

[*Wolf howls off.*]

DULIA [*starting*]: How the wolves howl! They know the cow[27] has calved. Is the pen shut, Father?

RAWAL [*nods*]: Safe bind – safe find. [*Into the darkness, shaking his fist.*] Ah, you bold grey beasts. If we had anything like a village hunter to protect us instead of old Buldeo, you wouldn't sing like that.

DULIA: No! Your scalps would be at Kanhiwara town, where the English live – all counted and paid for. I wish I were a man. I'd go out with a gun and get the Government reward for a wolf or two.

MESSUA: The Gods forbid. Remember how your brother said the same thing last year and – the Lame Tiger took him.

RAWAL: Yes – and here comes our old braggart who is always going to kill the Lame Tiger – to-morrow.

[*Enter* BULDEO, *peacocking with gun.*]

[*Roughly.*] Oh, Buldeo, my cow[28] calved this evening. The wolves seem to have news of it before thee. Art thou going to shoot a few of them?[29]

MESSUA [*to* DULIA]: Get him a pipe. That is what he has come for. [BULDEO *sits down and* DULIA *from clay fire-box puts a live charcoal ball on the pipe.* MOWGLI *and* MOTHER WOLF *show themselves in the grass behind, watching intently.*]

MOWGLI: So that is how the Red Flower is carried about! If such a little cub as that little white one can handle it, I have no fear.

MOTHER WOLF: I love thee, my son, but I do not love the Red Flower – and I do not love the man with the gun.

MOWGLI: It is only the old grey ape who goes a little way into our jungle, and runs out again when he sees Bagheera's trail. I have passed within touch of him a hundred times. He can neither see, nor hear, nor smell.

BULDEO [*impatiently above pipe*]:[30] Wolves? Wolves? There is not a wolf within miles of us. They know me by this time, and [*showing gun*] my wand[31] of office.

MOWGLI: See, oh see! It is the gun[32] that Baloo knocked out of his hand last moon, when he met him in the Jungle.[33] There are the marks of Baloo's claws[34] on it.

BULDEO: What is a mangy wolf here and there? Ever since I killed the black bear whose hide was so torn I could not bring it in, the Jungle knows Buldeo – yes. [*Puffs.*]

DULIA: And I mend the fence every day when the wild pig break in. *I* know Buldeo.

RAWAL [*ironically*]: We all know Buldeo.

BULDEO [*meditatively, with immense importance*]: And yet how heavy a thing is fame! Now, even in Kanhiwara, forty miles from here, the young English police officer says: – *Again* it is Buldeo who comes to claim the reward for killing a tiger.

MESSUA [*aside*]: Buldeo, who *claims* the reward for killing a tiger – at Kanhiwara – forty miles from here. [*Aloud, leaning against the door-jamb.*] Thou hast killed many tigers?

BULDEO [*twirling moustache*]: A few – a few. Here and there. I make no boast.

MESSUA: Hast thou yet claimed the reward for the Lame Tiger – the devil that killed my boy Nathoo last year. The English have put a hundred rupees on his head.

BULDEO [*uneasy pause*]: These things are not so easy – even to a Buldeo.

MESSUA: There is not a man in our village whose cattle he has not killed. The very children know his foot-marks when they go out with the buffaloes. Month after month he eats at our expense.

DULIA [*aside*]: While Buldeo eats and drinks and smokes at our expense.

BULDEO: I will cast a certain sure bullet and the village priests shall bless it. We are in the hands of the Gods. Even I cannot always kill dead every time. [*Oriental gestures of explanation.*]

RAWAL: But why not once in a year – or twice?

BULDEO: I do! I do! I am known even at Kanhiwara. Have patience!

MESSUA: What else can a woman have in this world? [*Leans wearily against door-post.*]

BULDEO [*wriggling*]: Money for one thing. Ye are not a poor couple . . . I am no more than a simple hunter, contented with little, but . . .

RAWAL: Ohe! [*Aside.*] But I do not think even money would move him. [*To* MESSUA.] He thinks we should not make the poor English, our masters, pay all the reward for the Lame Tiger.

BULDEO: A few rupees – from the hand of a friend – are always befitting, and good powder is not cheap these days. [*Aside.*] I wish I had not talked about the cursed Lame Tiger, but perhaps the money may frighten them. [*Aloud.*] Yes, a few rupees.

MESSUA: The Lame Tiger and the Jungle are always at our gates: but if money will move thee [*to* RAWAL *with passionate gesture*] what is money beside the hope of revenge?

BULDEO: A woman and a priest and a snake are bad things to dispute with. [*To* RAWAL.] As I said, I am a simple hunter –

RAWAL: I see thy simplicity. [*Pause.*] I will add a bullock or twenty rupees to the Government reward, that the English will pay for the hide of the Lame Tiger.

BULDEO: The silver for me. Money breeds swifter than cattle.

[*A wolf howls.*]

MESSUA: Oh shame! The very beasts mock thee while we bargain.

MOTHER WOLF: That is Grey Brother. Akela has missed his kill and the pack has turned against him. Get the Red Flower and come away.

MOWGLI [*fascinated*]: All in good time, Mother. This is a new trail to me; I will follow it a little way. [*Looks intently.*]

MOTHER WOLF: Why do thy eyes hunt that little white one?

MOWGLI: I do not know. [*Abstractedly.*] She is like the white blossom that comes in the spring grass.

BULDEO: It is to be well thought of. The Lame Tiger is no common beast and twenty rupees is not so much after all.

MESSUA [*hand on fore-arm*]: I will add to them my silver amulets. All I ask is the Lame Tiger's hide. [*Chink of silver amulets.*]

BULDEO [*aside*]: What a friend is every woman. She would send me to my death and never even wipe her eyes. [*Aloud.*] As to the Lame Tiger – and the money – and the bracelets –

[*Wolf howls.*]

MOTHER WOLF: Come away.

MOWGLI: Cry the hunting cry then: but not too loudly. I would not have the – little white one frightened. Wait till she puts down the fire-pot.

MESSUA: We are waiting your answer, O mighty hunter! Canst thou tempt him, daughter?

DULIA [*laughing*]: He does not like it! Well then, Buldeo, on the day that thou bringest in the Lame Tiger's head, I will be thy sixth wife – or seventh, is it? There! I and my dowry, seven bullocks, three milch-cows and –

BULDEO: The Gods forbid – not even for thy dowry. I know what comes of marrying children. I had sooner marry a wild cat.

DULIA: So we are both of one mind, for *I* would far sooner be carried off by any demon in the Jungle. [*Laughs and sets down fire-pot.*]

RAWAL: A wolf! Close outside the wall! By the calf-pen! Quick, Buldeo. The gun!

[*Business with* BULDEO's *long matchlock.*]

MOWGLI: Louder!

[MOTHER WOLF *gives tongue again, and* MOWGLI *comes forward to the fire-pot in the light of the fire, as* DULIA *drops it and turns to run.*]

BULDEO AND RAWAL [*running to the house*]: It is a spirit! Protect us from sorcery! A spirit!

MESSUA [*stretching out her arm*]: It is Nathoo! The shape of my son Nathoo! [*On her knees.*] My son! Oh my son! [MOWGLI *stoops to fire-pot.*] Ay, take light for thy path to the Gods.

DULIA [*triumphantly*]: Nay. It is not Nathoo. It is some Godling of the Woods. [*Falls at his feet.*]

[MOWGLI *looks at her curiously and tenderly, fingers a lock of her hair, picks up fire-pot and disappears.*]

Scene closes.

SCENE 3

The Council Rock by moonlight. AKELA's *seat is vacant.* WOLVES *ranged in semi-circle.* SHERE KHAN: BAGHEERA, *right. Enter* MOWGLI *with fire-pot.*

MOWGLI [*aside to* BAGHEERA]: It is here. I have seen men thrust dry sticks into it, and presently the Red Flower blossoms at the end. Look! [*Waves fire-pot.*]

BAGHEERA: Well hunted. We shall need it – if I know the Jungle. But keep it away from me. [*Flinches.*]

SHERE KHAN: Good hunting, man-cub.

[MOWGLI *turns his back.*]

TABAQUI: Good hunting, little ankle-bones. Hee! Hee! Silence! My Lord speaks.

[MOWGLI *stands contemptuously aside, blowing on fire-pot from time to time.* BAGHEERA *keeps behind* MOWGLI.]

SHERE KHAN: Free Hunters, ye know that to-night Akela has missed his kill. Therefore he dies –

WOLVES: By the Law, he dies!

SHERE KHAN: Since the leadership of the pack is open, and being asked to speak –

MOWGLI [*looking up from fire-pot with scornful puff*]: By whom? Are we all jackals to fawn on this cattle-butcher?

WOLVES: Silence, thou man-cub . . . No, let him speak.

THREE VOICES [*together*]: Let Akela speak.

SHERE KHAN: Let the dead wolf speak.

AKELA [*under the rock*]: Free People, and ye, oh jackals of Shere

Khan, I have missed my kill, as ye know, and by the Law I die.

WOLVES: Die then!

AKELA: It is your right to kill me at the Council Rock. But it is my right, by Jungle Law, that ye come one by one. [*Half rising.*] Therefore, I ask: who comes to make an end of Akela?

WOLVES [*uneasily, talking among themselves*]: Not I. Oh spring at his throat! Thou art stronger than he. [*Silence.*]

BAGHEERA [*politely*]: Wilt thou try, Shere Khan?

[MOWGLI *laughs.*]

SHERE KHAN: Let this toothless fool alone. He can lead the pack no more. It is the man-cub yonder who has lived too long. Free People, he was my meat from the first.

BAGHEERA: But thou didst not take him, eh?

SHERE KHAN: Give him to me. He has troubled the Jungle for twelve rains. He is a man – a man, and from the marrow of my bones I hate him.

[WOLVES *growl assentingly.*]

AKELA: Then let him go to his own place.

SHERE KHAN: To turn all the people of the village against us. He knows our lairs and our drinking pools. [*Growl from* WOLVES.] No, give him to me.

AKELA: He has eaten our food. He has slept with us. He has driven game for us. He has not broken the Jungle Law.

MOTHER WOLF: I am his Lair-Mother. He will live to slay thee yet, Lame One!

BALOO [*very insinuatingly*]: I do not love killing – I. But if the man-cub is to be killed, old Baloo will strike a blow or two on his side. [*Strikes the air.*]

BAGHEERA: Also, I paid the life of a bull for him when he was accepted. The worth of a bull is little, but Bagheera's honour in the Jungle is something for which he may perhaps fight.

WOLVES: A dead bull – years ago! What do we care for old dry bones?

BAGHEERA: Or for a pledge. Well are ye called the Free People!

SHERE KHAN: No man-cub can run with the people of the Jungle. Give him to me!

AKELA [*half rising*]: Hear me first! Some of ye, I know, have followed Shere Khan. Under his teaching ye go by night and snatch children from the villagers' doorsteps. So I know ye are cowards. It is to cowards I speak. Let the man-cub go to his own place and – I will die here without fighting. That will save at least three lives and it is very good to live.

MOWGLI [*clapping hands like a disinterested spectator*]: Well said, Lone Wolf. I promise thee thy life for this.

TABAQUI: Do not give what does not belong to thee, little ankle-bones.

AKELA: More I cannot do, but I can at least save ye the shame of killing a brother spoken for and brought into the pack according to the Law of the Jungle. Choose!

SHERE KHAN: He is a man – a man – a man!

[*Rising chorus of growls.*]

WOLVES: A man – a man – and he dies!

BAGHEERA: That is the death–note. Now the hunting is in thy hands, Little Brother.

[MOWGLI *moves forward.*]

TABAQUI: Do not be afraid, man-cub.

MOWGLI [*standing up. Stretches his arms and yawns*]: Listen you! Ye have told me so often I am a man (though indeed I would have been a wolf with you to my life's end) that I feel your words are true. So I do not call you brothers but dogs – dogs – as man should.

WOLVES: And we will slay thee now.

MOWGLI [*coldly*]: What ye will do and what ye will not do is not yours to say. It is with me, and that we may all see the matter more clearly, I, a man, have brought a little of the Red Flower which ye dogs fear. [*Thrusts torch into fire-pot. It blazes and beasts shrink back, muttering: – 'The Flower! The Red Flower! We cannot stand against the Red Flower! Ah! Take it away!'*]

MOWGLI [*stands gazing sardonically round circle*]: Good! I see that ye are dogs. [*Spits.*] I go from you this day to the man-pack. But I will be more merciful than you. Because I hunted and slept with you, I will not betray you to the man-pack as ye have betrayed me. But there is a debt to pay before I go. [*Crosses to* SHERE KHAN, *catches him by the throat*.] Stir a whisker, and I ram the Red Flower down thy gullet. [*To pack*.] This cattle-killer said he would kill me because I am a man. Thus, then, do we men beat dogs when we are angry. [*Beats* SHERE KHAN.] Pah! Singed Jungle-cat, go now. But remember the next time I come to the Council Rock, by the Bull that bought me, I will come with Shere Khan's hide, and lay it down here.

[SHERE KHAN *slinks off silently*.]

WOLVES: Have mercy, man-cub. Have mercy. Take away the Red Flower.

MOWGLI: Be silent. Hear my orders, dogs. Ye will *not* kill Akela, because I choose that he lives. Is that plain, or shall I light the long grass and smoke ye like bees? [*Pointing*.] Nor do I think ye shall sit here any longer, lolling out your tongues as though ye were somebody instead of dogs, whom I drive out thus! [*Beats* WOLVES *off: all except* MOTHER WOLF *and the four brothers. Sits down panting and sobs. To* BAGHEERA.] What is it? What is it? I do not wish to leave the Jungle. Why is my face wet? [*Sits down with face on knees*.]

BAGHEERA: That is only tears, such as men use. Now I know thou art a man, and a wolf-cub no longer. Man goes to man at last.

MOWGLI: And I loved them! They were my brothers! Why did they hate me?

GREY BROTHER [*approaching with three* WOLVES]: And we love thee. We are still thy brothers.

MOWGLI: Ye will not forget me – ye will not – [*Breaks down*.]

GREY BROTHER [*nose on knee*]: Never while we can follow a trail. Come to the edge of the fields and we will play with thee by moon light among the crops.

MOWGLI [*head on* MOTHER WOLF'*s neck*]: And thou, Lair-Mother?

MOTHER WOLF: There is my milk in thy blood. Thy heart beat next to mine o'cold nights in the lair. I lay between thee and the wrath of Shere Khan before thou couldst walk, child of man. I loved thee better than ever I loved my cubs . . . Eat, drink and be strong among the man-pack, and come soon to keep thy promise.

BALOO: I do not love killing, I – but come soon with the hide.

BAGHEERA: Learn man's cunning, Little Brother. There is no cunning can stand against it.

MOWGLI [*rising*]: I will surely come – I will come with Shere Khan's hide to the Council Rock; though now I go to the man-pack . . . Do not forget me in the Jungle. [*Exit.*]

TABAQUI [*in the bushes*]: *We* will not forget thee – Shere Khan and I. Ha! Ha! Ha!

ACT II

SCENE I

Outside MESSUA's *hut in the dawn:* MOWGLI *asleep on the edge of the high grass.* GREY BROTHER's *head pokes through the grass immediately above him.*

GREY BROTHER: So much for the three moons which he has spent with the man-pack. They have ruined him. He cannot hear or smell. He lets me creep up to his naked throat. Well for my brother that I love him.

MOWGLI [*without rising, catches* GREY BROTHER *by the throat and unsheathes his knife round his neck*]: Have I forgotten how to hear or smell? [*Flourishing knife.*] Now, what shall I do to thee?

GREY BROTHER: Well done! I was afraid three months with the man-pack had spoilt thy hand.

MOWGLI: Not yet. Where hast thou been ever since the wolf-pack cast me out?

GREY BROTHER: Following Shere Khan. There was need. [*Sits with head confidentially on* MOWGLI's *knee and* MOWGLI *flings an arm round it, picking off a burr here and there in the coat.*]

MOWGLI: Oho! Has the Lame Tiger's coat grown since I singed it?

GREY BROTHER: Yes, it has grown and his hate too. He hid himself for three months. *I* knew – but yesterday he crossed the ranges hot foot on thy trail. Tabaqui was with him.

MOWGLI [*biting back of forefinger thoughtfully*]: I am not afraid of Shere Khan, but Tabaqui is very cunning.

GREY BROTHER: I met Tabaqui an hour ago. Now he is telling his cunning to the kites, but before he died he told me all he knew. Shere Khan will catch thee at the village gates to-night when the cattle come in.

MOWGLI [*scornfully*]: As though I were an old woman. And where does he hide now?

GREY BROTHER: In the ravine by the river. He killed at midnight – a pig – and lies gorged on his meat. He will sleep till the shadows grow long.

MOWGLI: He has eaten and drunk and lies asleep! Is he tired of his wicked life that he comes to give it to me?

GREY BROTHER: How wilt thou take it? That little knife round thy neck can do him no harm.

MOWGLI: No-o. [*Fingers knife.*] But – I have not lived with the man-pack for nothing. It is Shere Khan's life or mine. Thou shalt see the end, Grey Brother.

GREY BROTHER: Good hunting! I do not fear for thy life now thou art warned. [*Looks round.*] Tell me something of this same man-pack. What like of breed are they at close grips?

MOWGLI: Not unlike the Monkey People. They are always giving tongue, and they never look at the trail. They are afraid of the darkness which brings *us* abroad, and they say the thing which is not* for jest or for the sake of food.

GREY BROTHER: That is the Monkey People to the last hair. But how have they dealt with thee?

MOWGLI: Very wonderfully. I have learned their speech and I can give tongue as loudly as any one of them. [*Points to a house.*] Now this tall trap is my lair, and they have given me a foster-father and a foster-mother – yes, and a cub to play with – a Little White One with a voice like water slipping between rocks in the Jungle on a hot night – far off.

GREY BROTHER: Then they knew thou wast a bold hunter and made thee welcome.

---

* Swift, *Gulliver's Travels*, Book 4, Chapter 3. This term for a lie does not occur in the *Jungle Books*; it is used four times in *The Jungle Play*.

MOWGLI [*loftily*]: Thou art only a wolf: thou dost not understand
men. It was because the woman, my foster-mother, missed a cub
of her own last rains, my size and shape. [*Points to himself.*] He
wandered into the Jungle and [*gesture*] Shere Khan took him. She
said that I – I [*laughs*] was that very cub come back from Shere
Khan's mouth. [*About here* MOWGLI *disengages himself from* GREY
BROTHER *and sits cross-legged before him, emphasizing his remark
with hand gestures.*]

GREY BROTHER: A man-cub that Shere Khan killed last rains? Why,
those white bones are in the thicket at the back of the river. We
have both seen them.

MOWGLI: Ay. All the Jungle knows it. [*Nods.*]

GREY BROTHER [*immensely interested, nose held level like dog-pointing*]:
So *she* said the thing which was not. Did she say it for a jest – or
for sake of food?

MOWGLI: Not for a jest because the water ran out of her eyes. Nor
for food, because she gave *me* food – hot food burned over the
Red Flower.

GREY BROTHER: Then she did not know her own cub. [*Pause, and
scratches himself.*] Perhaps a jackal had bitten her and it was the
madness.

MOWGLI: Ah, that was it. *I* never thought of that trail. Yes, it was
madness, because when she had asked me a hundred questions
about her cub which I could not answer –

GREY BROTHER [*proudly*]: His bones lying in the thicket: see, I do
understand men. [MOWGLI *smiles assentingly.*]

MOWGLI: She gave tongue before the whole man-pack, and said
that whether I were her cub or not –

GREY BROTHER: And thou art a wolf and the child of a wolf.

MOWGLI: She would be my foster-mother for the sake of that missing
cub.

GREY BROTHER: Good hunting! And what said the foster-father?

MOWGLI [*with gesture of contempt – shut hand opening quickly*]: Oh
he – he was her mate. He growled a little and followed her trail.

GREY BROTHER: Then the man-pack are like *us*. How do they kill?

MOWGLI: They do not kill. They dig in the dirt with sticks and eat

27

what grows up. They set great store on grain and fruit. But they do not know how to guard it. The woman, my foster-mother, was vexed when I came, because the deer ate their crops and the Monkey People ate their fruit. Also, the Little White One with a dove's voice told me that the wild pig rooted up the thorn fences about their fields. So I slipped out one night and schooled the deer and the swine and the Monkey People – I saw Akela and my Lair-Mother together in the moonlight. That night I ate clean flesh.

GREY BROTHER: Very good it is.

MOWGLI: It was a little thing, but since then the deer and the swine and the Monkey People have left our fields alone, and oh! Grey Brother, if thou could'st only hear the man-pack at evening giving tongue all together and marvelling how it was done. I sit among them and am near to bursting with mirth. There is an old dry thing with a gun who moves like a lame ox, who says that he guards the man-pack from *us*! From *us*!

GREY BROTHER: The grey ape that coughs and hawks about the edge of the Jungle?[1] Bent – with white hair,[2] and smells like a musk-rat?

MOWGLI: Ay, Buldeo. That is the vermin's very name. He does not at all love me, because I laugh when he tells the man-pack tales about *us*. By the Bull that bought me, I have never heard such monkey-stories. He cannot see a trail before him more than a day old; he cannot tell a wolf's foot from a jackal's; he cannot smell; he cannot hear; and *he* is called a hunter! Yes, *he* has frightened the deer and the swine and the monkeys from the fields; and he will presently kill Shere Khan.

GREY BROTHER: Little Brother, hast thou learned to say the thing that is not?

MOWGLI: Indeed no. This Buldeo man hunts Shere Khan every day – very loudly – with his mouth – just as the Monkey People hunt *us* – from a safe high branch.

GREY BROTHER: Oho! Tell him then that he has hunted me and my three brothers in the same fashion.

MOWGLI: He will tell that tale fast enough – in his own fashion. When was it?

GREY BROTHER: Last night. We found him on the edge of the Jungle, blowing smoke out of his mouth, and he fled up a tree, dropping his gun. So, being idle, we e'en sat down and sang a song to cheer him till the moon rose. I heard his teeth chatter like a porcupine's quills. Does he not love thee, Little Brother? Then next time I will bring thee his head.

MOWGLI: Men do not kill men. Let him live. He hurts nothing. It is Shere Khan we must bring to the death. Listen! My hunting with this man-pack is to go out with the buffaloes every day, and to guard them while they graze, lest any of us [*chuckles*] – lest any bold wicked beast of the Jungle should kill them.

GREY BROTHER: But not even Shere Khan would spring at a herd of buffaloes together. It is sure death! A calf here and there, may be – but a herd – no!

MOWGLI [*laughing*]: I am telling thee the wisdom of the man-pack. Meet me with Akela and one or two of the brethren on the flats by the Waingunga an hour hence, and I will show thee *Mowgli's* wisdom. [*Taps head.*] It is all here.

GREY BROTHER: And perhaps thou wilt give us one little goat, if we –

MOWGLI: No, Brother. Were the goats mine, we would kill now, but they belong to the man-pack which feeds me [*aside*] and the Little White One loves them.

GREY BROTHER: This is a new Mowgli to me. There is a look in thy eyes. There are new words on thy tongue. I am – I do not understand – but I love thee, man or wolf, I love thee. [*Anxiously.*] Do not forget thou art a wolf, Little Brother.

MOWGLI: Never; but I will also remember that I have been cast out of the wolf-pack.

GREY BROTHER: And that thou mayst be cast out of the man-pack, too. Wolves are wolves, but men are men. [*Conch blows in temple.*] Thy man-pack are stirring. I go. In an hour, then, I will meet thee with Akela and the Brethren. [*Exit.*]

MOWGLI [*calling off*]: Ay, on the plain, by the ravine, and we will trample Shere Khan as flat as a frog in a drought. [*Takes stage, half holding out arms.*] Oh, my Brother, my Brother, and the good nights in the Jungle! [*Turns to house as village wakes.*] But this is my lair now, and it is good here also. [*Looks round him.*] If Shere Khan had not taken Messua's boy, he would to-day rejoice in the sunlight and the faces of his kin. [*Thinks it over: shakes his head.*] For myself I might almost have spared Shere Khan, but – no. He took Messua's boy – the Little White One's brother. I will give Shere Khan to the kites before noon. Foolish – foolish beasts!

[MESSUA, DULIA, *and* RAWAL *come out of the hut.*]

MESSUA: Wilt thou never learn man's ways? Sleeping in the open brings fever.

[RAWAL *comes to left to mend plough and kneels over it.*]

DULIA: Yes, and a beast of the night might carry thee off, and then the wild pig would break into our millet again. How dost thou keep them out, Mowgli?

MOWGLI [*laughing: prepares sticks for fire*]: Oh, I shout at them, and they understand.

MESSUA: That is one of his fairy stories. He said the same to me when the monkeys stopped stealing our fruit, because they were sick.

MOWGLI [*aside: handing stick to* DULIA]: Yes, the Monkey People were very sick. [*To* MESSUA.] Hot cakes, Mother, and a handful of dried grain. I must go out with the buffaloes.[3]

MESSUA [*preparing pipe for her husband*]: Hot cakes there shall be, my son. Now, my boy Nathoo, that was taken by the Lame Tiger, always said, when he saw hot cakes . . . But perhaps thou can'st remember what he said. [*Voice breaks a little.*]

DULIA [*aside over fire*]: Pity her. *I* know thou art not Nathoo.

MOWGLI [*lifting arms*]: Hai, my Mother! Was thy son all marked with the scars of old bites? Were his feet as hard as flint? Was he dumb? – as I was when I came here three months ago, and thou didst give me a place by the fire.

MESSUA [*tenderly*]: And a place in my heart too. I know it; thou art not my son, Nathoo, but women always love to cheat themselves.

RAWAL [*smoking*]: What folly! Anyone could see he is no more Nathoo than a wild buffalo is a milch-cow.

MESSUA: But I love him as though he were my son – almost. And, remember, my husband, there has certainly been a blessing on

30

the homestead since we took him in. [*Earnestly.*] And canst thou never remember thy mother?

MOWGLI: No, my Mother.

MESSUA: Ai! Poor mother! The Gods pity all us women!

RAWAL [*above pipe, slowly*]: Yes, the boy was worth adopting. He is cheap too. He has not lost a single calf since he took them grazing. Some day, if he works well, I will give him a young calf, perhaps a goat,[4] that he may make merry with his friends.

MOWGLI [*smiling and squatting down, as* MESSUA *hands him a cake*]: That I may make merry with my friends. I must take care not to lose a goat now.

[*Enter* BULDEO *with gun and three* VILLAGERS.]

BULDEO: Delay me not! Delay me not! A draught of milk, then, and one pull at the pipe. [*Sits down:* DULIA *brings milk.*] Who hunts the Lame Tiger has no time to waste.

MOWGLI: The old lie – the old gun –[5] Faugh! It is time I made an end of Shere Khan, if only for Buldeo's sake.

FIRST VILLAGER: If I ploughed as Buldeo hunts, I should be sold to the money-lender in a week.

SECOND VILLAGER: Ah! But where should we be without Buldeo?

THIRD VILLAGER: And his Lame Tiger . . . [*To* BULDEO.] What hast thou done *this* time, O Father of Nimrod?

BULDEO: Ye may mock. I have tracked him at last. I tracked him last night.

MOWGLI: Last night? . . . Oh yes. He is as shameless as a monkey. Here comes the tale. [*Soberly to* DULIA.] Listen to this, Dulia.[6] [*Gets up, stuffs cake in his mouth and goes over to* VILLAGERS.]

BULDEO [*snarling as he goes by*]: Time for thee to herd the buffaloes,[7] wolf's brat.

MOWGLI [*feigning fear*]: But if the Lame Tiger is hereabouts, it is not safe for me to go out with them.[8]

BULDEO: Little coward! When the very deer and pig and monkeys are afraid to approach the fields. [*To* VILLAGERS.] Ye may have noticed that last night I came home late. [MOWGLI *laughs.*] Mannerless wolf's brat! I had found the Lame Tiger asleep under a tree. [MOWGLI *laughs again.*]

MESSUA: Do not vex him, Mowgli.

BULDEO [*louder*]: I said I found him and shot him twice. Then I followed the blood-trail till the light fell. That is the reason I came home so late. [*Points.*] Why does not that kinless whelp go to work?

FIRST VILLAGER: Now ten or even five years ago I should have said that was great news . . . but, somehow Brethren, one gets older [*scratching his head*], and – and – one goes off ploughing just the same. [*Exit* FIRST VILLAGER.]

SECOND VILLAGER: *I* think the Lame Tiger is a ghost – our Buldeo is always tracking him and wounding him to the death and next week – tck! – there's another of our bullocks dead.[9]

MOWGLI: I know the Lame Tiger is a lazy coward: but the people who hunt him are worse. That is all.

BULDEO: That is all, is it? To mock me before thy elders. If I were Rawal, I would beat thee within an inch of thy life. What dost thou know of hunting, boy-without-caste?

[MOWGLI *smiles very calmly.*]

DULIA [*angrily*]: Enough to keep the wild pig out of our fields, which *thou* couldst never do.

MESSUA: And the monkeys from our fruit.

BULDEO [*furiously*]: And *this* is the reward of my night-watching and hard lying. One would think he were the village hunter himself, and not a wastrel cattle-herd.

RAWAL: He is a mannerless boy, but the village knows he is a good herdsman with the buffaloes. [*To* VILLAGERS.] He has not lost a single calf.

SECOND VILLAGER: But Buldeo does not love him.

THIRD VILLAGER: That is quite true. The boy is always laughing at his tales.

BULDEO: *I* am not a cattle-herd, drowzing in the sun. I am a hunter. The English know me at Kanhiwara. [*Puffs gloriously.*]

MOWGLI: And they know thee in the Jungle too. What were the reasons that kept thee in the tree till moonrise last night? [BULDEO *starts.*] Did they sing well, Buldeo? [*Significant gesture of the wolf's leap. Semi-circle of right-arm, hand opening and shutting.*]

BULDEO: There was not a wolf in sight, thou sorcerer. I say I shot the Lame Tiger.

MOWGLI: From a tree-top without thy gun – a good shot. [*Laughs.*] Oh Buldeo, thou wilt be the death of me some day with thy trackings and thy shootings, and thy frightenings of deer and pig, and thy owl's face on it all!

BULDEO: Am I to be made a mock of by children? [*Aside.*] How could he have known? This comes of fostering wolf-brats from the Jungle. [*Aloud.*] Forty years have I hunted and killed beasts and . . . and . . .

MOWGLI: Three months have I lived in this village and I do not remember thou hast ever spoken one true word about one beast, or bird, or track, or trail, or manner, or custom of the beasts in all the Jungle.

[MESSUA *puts up hand restrainingly.* DULIA *nods approval.*]

DULIA [*aside*]: I can well believe it.

RAWAL: This is beyond a jest. He is an old man. Be silent, Mowgli.

BULDEO [*burbling with wrath*]: I will not bandy words with a wolf-brat – a Jungle-thing – a gipsy – a – a – brother of dogs. We will speak to the village elders this evening, and perhaps a little beating with a plough-beam may teach this master of woodcraft something.

[*Exit* BULDEO *with* VILLAGERS.]

MOWGLI [*still laughing*]: It is true – all true, though – beating or no beating. He has neither shame, nor sight, nor smell. Oh if he knew. [*Overcome with laughter.*]

MESSUA: Thou art a graceless scamp, but [*aside*] it is just as my son Nathoo would have spoken . . . but [*looking round yard*] – off to work, my men. I have my hands full with the housework.

RAWAL: And thou must go out with the herd.

MOWGLI [*picking up sticks in corner*]: True. They have a hard day before them.

RAWAL: What? Is the grazing poor?[10] Do not venture too near the edge of the Jungle, then. Dulia, thou must not leave the village to-day . . . Buldeo is something of a liar, but he may have seen the Lame Tiger after all. I must get to my ploughing. [*Picks up plough and pipe and exits.*]

DULIA: Oh, and I meant to bring[11] thee thy noon-meal, Mowgli.

MOWGLI: Best not to-day. [*Half aloud.*] But I should like to have shown it thee.

DULIA: What, hast thou – a gift?

MOWGLI: Yes – a little gift.

DULIA: A rush ring – a necklace of seeds – a cage full of fighting grasshoppers – what? Oh tell me.

MOWGLI [*pacing it out*]: Only three – may be four paces of painted hide – a little mangy on the back and shoulders.

DULIA: For me?

MOWGLI: No, not for thee. For my friends.

DULIA: But we are thy friends, my mother, my father and I.

MOWGLI: I know it. But this is for my enemies also.[12]

DULIA: For Buldeo? He hates thee enough.

MOWGLI: Oh, Buldeo is all long tail and loud talk, like Mao the peacock. No, I shall *not* give it to him.

DULIA: Then he will do thee an injury . . . Ah, tell me for whom is thy gift, and I will scratch her eyes out.

MOWGLI: The Jungle forbid,[13] unless I were near. [*Aside.*] Those hands in Akela's eyes or Bagheera's . . . [*Aloud.*] Thou hast been my playmate for three moons, Dulia. There is very little I would not tell thee except [*shakes his head*] – the names of my friends.

DULIA: No matter. I will come some day and spy upon you all – you and your friends.

MOWGLI: Oh, that is very easy. Behind the river lies a certain great rock, which was my throne in the days when I was a prince.

DULIA: Another silly fairy tale. I am *not* a child to be treated so. I am almost a woman!

MOWGLI [*jestingly*]: Do not be angry, oh woman. It is the very rock I showed thee once far off on a hill. Come thither by night.

DULIA: Not to be eaten by wolves. Go along to thy buffaloes.

MOWGLI: Come singing that little song I taught thee when I first learnt to speak man's talk, and no beast[14] will hurt thee. [DULIA *pouts.*] Then thou shalt see my friends. That is *not* fairy tale.[15]

DULIA [*coquettishly*]: Mowgli, thou art an ill-conditioned wolf-cub as Buldeo says – and if I did not love to play with thee, and to hear thy wonderful fairy tales of the beasts, I would hate thee. Go along with thy stupid[16] buffaloes, and may thou be frightened – just a little frightened – by the Lame Tiger. [*Runs after.*] But, oh Mowgli, do not run risk.[17] Do not get a hurt. If thou seest him, run. Promise!

MOWGLI: Yes. When I see the Lame Tiger I promise I will run. I will run hard. [*Goes out with stick, crying: 'Up bulls. Up bulls of the herd!'*]

SCENE 2

The ravine by the Waingunga. Enter MOWGLI *with* AKELA. *He has a long stick in his hand and is dressed as a herdsman.*

AKELA: Now how do we hunt, man-cub? Remember Shere Khan is not a buck and I am not a wolf.

MOWGLI [*meditatively*]: Hm! Yonder is the ravine where Shere Khan sleeps.

AKELA: And heavily. Chil the Kite watches him.

MOWGLI: Good, and the sides of the ravine are higher than he can climb, even if he were empty.

AKELA: True; but how does that help us?

MOWGLI: Wait a little, old hunter. [*Points off.*] Yonder are the buffaloes. I have divided the bulls from the cows. Grey Brother will drive the bulls slowly to the head of the ravine, where it is steep. Thou wilt drive the cows to the foot of it where it comes out into the plain. [*Damps finger and holds it up.*] Which way is the wind?

AKELA: Art thou losing thy nose in the man-pack?

MOWGLI: I have learnt men's cunning. So soon as the bulls wind Shere Khan they will charge upon him down the ravine, and before he is well awake, they will trample him flat. He cannot spring aside, and if he runs away from the bulls –

AKELA: He meets the cows at the foot of the ravine, and they will fight for their calves. He is in a trap.[18] Oh, man's cunning indeed!

MOWGLI: Aha. *Now* thou seest. [*Waves hand*.] Off then and herd thy cows. I will sit here and call[19] the hunting.

[*Exit* AKELA. MOWGLI *drops his cloak, and begins in a low voice turning alternately left and right, hand shading forehead against sun glare, waving with right hand and as the interest quickens, grasping his knife*.] Softly, softly, Akela. That cow will break back if she is pressed. [*To cows*.] Softly, my pretty ones. Let the calves keep with them. [*Left, where* GREY BROTHER *is working*.] Let Rama the herd-bull lead, Grey Brother. Let Rama the herd-bull lead,[20] and the rest will follow him. Do not jump at his nose, or he will charge thee all down the ravine.[21] Run before him to the head of the ravine. [*A pause. Excitedly calling*.] Do not let them scatter among the rocks. Send a brother out to the left flank of the bulls.[22] Soo! Soo! [*Right; to* AKELA.] Oh, well done, Akela. Thou art better than fifty herdsmen. Drive the cows a little further up the ravine. What is it?[23]

AKELA: The wind has shifted. A cow has winded him here. She begins to paw. Are the bulls up?

MOWGLI: All but. [*Signalling left*.] Be swift, Grey Brother! Nip their flanks! Up! Up! Up! To the head of the ravine. Drive them up!

GREY BROTHER [*far away*]: Now the bulls have winded him. They are making sure of the scent. [*Pause, as* MOWGLI *stiffens and stands up, hands to mouth*.] Now! Wake Shere Khan! Wake!

SHERE KHAN [*off*]: Who calls?

MOWGLI: I, Mowgli, cattle-thief! Man-killer! It is time to come to the Council Rock. Down! Drive the bulls down, Grey Brother! Hold thy cows steady, Akela. [*Looking down into ravine*.] Hai! The charge of the buffaloes! What tiger can stand against that! Well done, Rama. Well done, Bull of the herd! Nay – not that way, Shere Khan. The sides are too steep to climb. Run – for thy life run! The bulls are on him. Horn and hoof together! Fight, then, Shere Khan. He is too gorged even to lift a paw! He goes under like a log in a flood and here come the cows! [*Leans forward, face set*.] It is I – I – I that did this. Remember Mowgli, the frog. Remember the man-cub last rains. White bones in the thicket by the Waingunga! [*Gesture*.] Ah! Too soon! He is dead. There is not a whole bone in his carcass. And the herd has gone mad with the blood scent. Quick, Akela. Quick, Brethren. Break them up! Scatter them on the plain again, or they will be goring one another. Hai! Hai! Hai! Gently, my pretty ones. Oh, they will spoil the hide. [*Leaps down behind rock with stick.*]

[*Here comes tableau of death shown for a moment. Quick curtain, and* MOWGLI *is revealed standing over* SHERE KHAN'*s limp body.* GREY BROTHER *and* AKELA *by his side.*]

GREY BROTHER [*panting*]: Wah! That was a dog's death for a dog. Man's cunning. Who shall stand against it?

AKELA [*sniffing carcass*]: So that debt is paid now.

MOWGLI: Not quite. I must lay his hide out on the Council Rock! So! [*Sharpens knife and stoops to carcass, but checks himself.*]

AKELA: What is it, man-cub?

MOWGLI: I cry my kill according to the Law of the Jungle.

GREY BROTHER: But thou art a man.

MOWGLI: Not this little while. Suffer me to remember the old days. [*Throwing back his hair and looking up.*] Ehu-yah! Alu! Lu! To the High and the Low Jungle – to the wings, to the beaks, to the claws, to the cleansers of the ways – to the choosers of the Slain – to Chil the Kite and the children of Tabaqui the Jackal, here is meat! Full gorge – full gorge! – My kill! My kill! My kill!

AKELA: He remembers well.

GREY BROTHER: Listen! Chil is always hungry.

[*Music.*]

This was my companion going out to fight
    For Chil – look you, for Chil.
Now come I to whistle him the ending of the fight.
    Chil – vanguards of Chil!
Word he gave me underfoot of quarry newly slain
Word I gave him overhead of buck upon the plain –
Here's an end of every trail – he shall not hunt again.*

[*A pause.*]

* Adapted from the first seven lines of 'Chil's Song', following 'Red Dog' in *The Second Jungle Book*.

37

MOWGLI: But why does not the old scavenger come down? All is ready.

GREY BROTHER: He sees further than we do. [*Sniffs*.] Man! And if I have not lost my nose it is the same old Buldeo we treed* last night. Phew! Thou hast called up a scavenger indeed!

MOWGLI: Ah, Buldeo – a very clever hunter. He has promised me some beating.

AKELA: Give me the word, and I will bring thee his head.

[MOWGLI *shakes his head*.]

GREY BROTHER: Let me smoke him[24] again.

MOWGLI: He is not worth even a jest.[25] Get to cover, and[26] we shall see what he says when he finds the Lame Tiger.

[*Enter* BULDEO *somewhat cautiously with gun*.]

BULDEO: Not yet noon, and the buffaloes have run back to the village gates mad with fear. So much for friend Rawal's pet herdsman who never lost a head! I do not love that brat, but if the Lame Tiger has by any chance picked him up, I think I can forgive him his beating, though he made an open jest of me this morning. But how did he know about my last night's little affair with the wolves up the tree? That was pure wickedness – ravens will peck out his eyes for it, but I'd sooner the Lame Tiger took him first. [*Catches sight of carcass*.] A-ah!

MOWGLI: Old Bat's-Eyes sees the kill at last.

BULDEO: The Gods protect me! Must I always climb trees? [*Cautiously*.] Blood on his muzzle! One paw doubled under him . . . He must have – [*Pokes very cautiously with gun*.] – He is – it is the Lame Tiger -- dead.

MOWGLI [*in the thicket*]: Alive or dead, he is a most prudent man – Buldeo.

BULDEO: Not a bullet mark on him . . . But there will be soon . . . There will be soon. I told the village I shot him twice . . . Two bullet marks . . . Of course I shot him. Of course I followed the blood-trail and finished him. Even the wolf's brat will believe me now. Oh Buldeo, thou art favoured by the Gods! [*Brings down gun*.][27]

---

* The typescript has 'freed'.

MOWGLI [*stepping forward*]: Heh, old man, do not spoil my skin.

BULDEO [*starting*]: Again the wolf-brat who sees things that do not happen – or at least that never should happen. Well, I shall be upsides with him. [*To* MOWGLI.] A pretty herdsman thou art! The buffaloes are gone back to the village. I come out to protect them, and I find thee – doing nothing. That means another beating.

MOWGLI [*to* WOLVES]: Lie still. [*With exaggerated penitence.*] I am sorry I do nothing.

BULDEO [*aside*]: He must have been sleeping in the shade, and he doesn't know. [*Aloud, relenting.*] Well, well, this time I am disposed to be lenient, since I have come upon the Lame Tiger whom, as I said, I wounded twice yesterday. Run back to the village with the news. I will shew thee the bullet holes when I have skinned him, and perhaps I will give thee a rupee out of the Government reward on his head. [*Pompously.*] A whole rupee – to buy sweets with. [*Brings matchlock down again. All through this dialogue* BULDEO *is absorbed in loading and priming his gun.*]

MOWGLI [*laughing*]: But how if I happen to need the skin for my own use?

BULDEO: What mad talk is this? Does a Buldeo track and slay tigers for a Mowgli to skin? I will not give thee one anna of the reward, only a big beating. It is beyond endurance. A Jungle-brat,[28] who does not know his own father's name! By the Gods, who are thy people under heaven that thou darest to open thy mouth against me?

MOWGLI [*with gesture to* AKELA]: These!

[AKELA *leaps from thicket, knocks over* BULDEO *and stands over him.* BULDEO *yells and lies still.*]

MOWGLI: Lie very still. Perhaps I may remember my father's name in a little. Perhaps I may even send my mother on a message to thee. [*Goes to carcass and sharpens knife: kneels.*] No-o! Thou art right. Thou wilt never give me one anna of the reward. There is an old war between this tiger and myself – a very old war – and I have won. That is all. [*To* AKELA.] We have a whole day's hard work here to strip the hide.

BULDEO: He wages war with tigers. Wolves are his servants. Ah! Now I understand how he knew of last night's mishap. A malignant and a pestilent sorcerer. I was right. I was right from the first. I suspected it when he mocked me. It is Jungle-magic. Only let me get back safe to the village, and if bullets blessed by the priest can do anything, he shall have the warmest welcome.

AKELA: This thing has an evil eye and it talks between its teeth. Let me bring thee the head.

MOWGLI [*stretching and yawning*]: I have killed once to-day.

AKELA: But its eyes are like Shere Khan's. It is old and wicked. Have a care.

BULDEO [*quaveringly*]: Great King – Ma-aster of Wolves –

MOWGLI [*chuckling; with skinning-knife tickling own palm*]: Oh-o! Where has the Jungle-brat gone – the kinless beggar – the wolf's spawn?

BULDEO: I am an old man. I – I did not know thou wast anything more than a herd-boy. Forgive me. Thou wilt not kill a harmless old man? May I go away or will thy servant tear me in pieces?

MOWGLI: Thou hast hunted beasts for forty years. Who am I to advise such a hunter?[29] [*Laughs.*] Oh if the village could only see thee, Buldeo. Shall I fetch them?

BULDEO [*aside*]: Then he does not mean to kill me at least. [*Aloud.*] In mercy – no. I – I am a very old man, and . . . perhaps, not over-truthful. I – I – I – did not know thee when I called thee names.

MOWGLI:[30] It is forgiven, because thou hast eaten and drunk from the hand of the Little White One.[31] Only another time[32] do not meddle with my kill. Let him rise, Akela.

AKELA: With those evil eyes shining?[33]

MOWGLI: I have said it. Go[34] in peace, Buldeo.[35] Some day, perhaps I will show thee a little real hunting. Go back to the village; tell them I have killed the Lame Tiger, and will bring in the hide by evening.

BULDEO: That I will assuredly do. Most assuredly. [*Aside.*] And I'll show[36] him a little real hunting there[37] if I can get a steady rest for my gun. [*Picks it up and exits.*]

AKELA: What is the sense of killing one Shere Khan and letting another go?[38] I saw hate, like a snake coiled, far back in his eyes. Even now, I can run after him, and bring thee his head.

MOWGLI: No. Let us get to the skinning. Remember I am also of the man-pack, and men do not kill men. [*Laughs.*][39]

Scene closes.

SCENE 3

The village gates at twilight. These stand half open. BULDEO *with his gun, the village* PRIEST, *and two* VILLAGERS *armed with spears, stand before them.* MESSUA, RAWAL *and* DULIA *are on the walls.*

VOICES [*intoning a prayer*[40]]: We are a little people, weak and afraid, living close to the Jungle, whence comes all evil by day and by night. Hear us, oh known and comfortable Gods of the hearth and the fields: protect us, Gods of the good ploughed land and the home altars: protect us against the ghosts and devils of the Jungle. For we are afraid – we are afraid – we are afraid! [VOICES *die down.*]

PRIEST: He is late. Are the stones ready?

BULDEO: Yes: and three slugs in my gun.

MESSUA [*from the wall, scornfully*]: Have a care! If he be such a sorcerer as Buldeo says, he may walk invisible.

PRIEST: I remember now his step was always light. But I have said prayers all round the village. He cannot break that spell.

DULIA: And thus ye reward one who has done you no harm but good.[41] Cowards!

BULDEO: Harm! I say again that scores of wolves leap out of the Jungle at his bidding. Even I could not prevail against them; though I slew and wounded many. They knocked me down, but they dared not eat me. They were afraid. Then that same innocent Mowgli turned himself into a tiger and danced on his hind legs. He is a wizard[42] – a ghost bringing evil.

MESSUA: I know thee of old, Buldeo, for a liar in grain. Not one word of this do I believe.

BULDEO: Be silent. We will reward thee later for fostering a wolf's brat [*aside*], who mocks good hunters.

VOICES: Yes. Listen to Buldeo. Messua and Rawal have brought calamity on the village. We are poor people! We will not have demons for herd-boys. Why did Messua feed the wolf's brat? It is the ghost of her boy Nathoo – possessed by the spirit of a tiger. We are afraid!

[*A wolf howls off. Silence for ten seconds.*]

VOICES [*intoning within*]: A spirit – an evil spirit – in league with the wolves – the grey wolf of the twilight – has taken the shape of a man. He has worked with us and bewitched men and women to love him. We will do justice on those that have trafficked with devils and given caresses to malignant ghosts! Forgive us, Gods of the Homestead!

BULDEO: Let him come nearer, and I can get a better shot . . .

MESSUA: Mowgli! Mowgli! Have a care.

BULDEO: Club her, bind her – gag her! She is in league with the wolf's brat.

A VOICE: Let her speak! Tell him to go away, Messua.

DULIA: Stop! They mean to[43] kill thee, Mowgli.

[*Enter* AKELA. BULDEO, PRIEST *and* VILLAGERS *hurry into gate, which shuts with a clang.* VILLAGERS *climb wall, shouting:* – 'Sorcerer! Wolf's brat! Jungle-devil! Ghost! Shoot, Buldeo, shoot!' *as* MOWGLI *enters with* SHERE KHAN's *hide on his head. A shower of stones follows.*]

MOWGLI: Now what is this? What have I done?

GREY BROTHER [*sitting down composedly*]: They are not unlike the wolf-pack, these brothers of thine. It is in my head they mean to cast thee out.

[BULDEO *shoots.*]

AKELA: Man does not kill man. Eh, Little Brother? Thou must have done them a kindness.

MOWGLI: I killed the Lame Tiger but – but –

BULDEO: Wolf-cub! Go away! Get back to thy people! I'll show thee a little hunting!

MOWGLI [*calling*]: Are ye all mad within there? I bring the Lame
   Tiger's hide. Look at it!

MESSUA [*from the wall*]: He has avenged my boy's death, and ye
   stone him. Let me go to him![44]

RAWAL: Stop the woman! Stop her! . . . or at least stop stoning the
   boy.

   [MESSUA *steps through gate and runs to* MOWGLI *and flings her arms
   round him.*]

MESSUA: Oh, my son! My son! they say thou art a sorcerer who can
   turn himself into a beast at will –

PRIEST: Tell him to go away, Messua.

MESSUA: I do not believe it, but go away or they will kill thee.
   Buldeo says thou art a wizard, but I know he lies!

PRIEST: Quick, Messua! Or we will stone thee with him.

MOWGLI [*laughing bitterly*]: Run back, Messua. I am no wizard, but
   I have paid thy debt – and a debt of my own to boot. [*Raises hand
   to mouth.*] They have struck me on the mouth and drawn blood.

GREY BROTHER: That grey ape gets ready to shoot again. I shall
   bring him down by the throat.

MOWGLI: No! Back, both of you. Farewell, Messua! [*Raising voice.*]
   Is the Little White One there?

   [MESSUA *runs back and a stone flies.*]

DULIA: I am here! Here, Mowgli!

VOICES: Club her! Knock her down! They are all in league with the
   wolf's brat.

MOWGLI: Be silent, or I will send in my servants to fetch me your
   lying tongues. [*Silence.*] Dulia – Little White One – am I a wizard?

DULIA: No! Thou art a man, and these men here are dogs.

MOWGLI: That is enough. I go back to my Jungle. Listen, man
   folk![45] Your bread is bitter and your water is muddy. I will be
   your herdsman no more. The buffaloes are over yonder. I have
   stolen none of them[46] . . .

VOICES: Go away! Get back to the Jungle!

AKELA: Take a head or two. At least take the old man's. I warned
   thee.

DULIA: Mowgli, oh Mowgli! they will do us an evil here. Whither dost thou go, Mowgli! Remember the Rock – the Rock and the Song.

MESSUA [*from wall*]: My son! My son! Wolf-brat or demon – I love thee – I love thee.

MOWGLI [*to village*]: Thank Messua that I do not come in with my wolves and hunt ye up and down your streets. Farewell. [*To* AKELA.] Well. *That* trail is finished. No more sleeping in houses for me. Let us away to the Council Rock.

GREY BROTHER: Better so. Ay, come back to the Jungle and lead the pack.

MOWGLI: Nay. Man-pack and wolf-pack have cast me out. Henceforward I will be the man alone.[47]

[*Exeunt.*]

VOICES [*intoning*]: Cleanse the altars! By fire we will cleanse the altars! Lest unwittingly we have done a wrong to the Home Gods! Spare us and our children, born and unborn, O Gods of the village. Spare the cattle and the crops and the houses till we make sacrifice of the evildoers that have brought ghosts and devils among us. [VOICES *die down*.]

ACT III

SCENE I

The Council Rock by moonlight. SHERE KHAN*'s hide on the Rock.* MOWGLI *standing on it.* BAGHEERA *and* BALOO *with* WOLVES *grouped below.* AKELA *and* GREY BROTHER *to left and right of hide.*

[*Music off.*]

What of the hunting, hunter bold?
    Brother, the watch was long and cold.
What of the quarry ye went to kill?
    Brother, he crops in the Jungle still.
What of the power that made thy pride?
    Brother, it ebbs from my flank and side.
What is your haste that ye hurry by?
    Brother, I go to my lair to die.*

AKELA: Look! Look well, oh wolves! The man-cub keeps his promise. Shere Khan is dead – is dead – is dead!

MOWGLI: Look well, O wolves! It is the hide of Shere Khan. I have killed him. I have kept my promise.

WOLVES: It is the hide of Shere Khan. The man-cub keeps his promise. We were lonely in the Jungle without thee.

---

* Chapter heading from 'Tiger! Tiger!' (*The Jungle Book*), with variants in the fifth and seventh lines.

MOTHER WOLF: Well-hunted, my son! I said on the night he first roared for thy blood that thou wouldst kill him.

MOWGLI: But for Akela and Grey Brother I could have done nothing. Oh Mother, Mother, if thou hadst seen the great bulls trample him flat[1] . . . Wow! That was good hunting! [*Hand to mouth.*] And then the man-pack threw stones at me.

MOTHER WOLF: I am glad I did not see that. I would have taken a heavy price from the man-pack, but I would have spared the woman, thy foster-mother –

BALOO: Peace, peace, Mother Wolf! Our man-cub comes back again, so wise that we must all lick his feet: and what is a cut or two on the head! It will teach him to leave men alone.[2]

AKELA: Leave men alone! Stay with us.

BAGHEERA [*aside*]: They are a restless pack[3] – men. *I* know something of the breed.

MOTHER WOLF: Yes. It is good in the Jungle – these long warm nights.

MOWGLI [*squatting on hide*]: It was good too in the man-pack, when the hot cakes smoked on the fires and we talked together at twilight.

BAGHEERA: And then they cut thy mouth with stones and tried to shoot thee. That was good hunting – eh?

MOWGLI: No – but only three months ago some wolves under that rock howled for my life . . . was that good hunting – eh! [*Abstractedly.*] And there was a girl in the pack who called me brother. We used to watch the buffalo grazing.

GREY BROTHER: *Watch* buffaloes! That was no hunting! Remember I showed thee how to work thy first kill.

MOWGLI [*hand closing on knife*]: Yes. A little fawn it was, and we fought over the carcass. I carry the mark of thy teeth on my thigh still.[4] [*Laughing.*] Oh, the old hot days in the Jungle, Grey Brother.

BALOO: And now thou hast returned, they will come again. Let the Jungle content thee. Leave men alone.

MOWGLI: I have nothing to love them for but – [*sighs*] – I am two Mowglis now. One Mowgli remembers how the wolf-pack cast him out, and the other Mowgli remembers how the man-pack cast him out . . . Dulia will gather sticks for the fire alone to-night . . . Ahai! [*Drops head between knees.*]

MOTHER WOLF [*to* GREY BROTHER]: Why does he do that? Is he hungry?

BAGHEERA: I know something of men, Mother Wolf. They are gay without reason, even when they have not killed. Without reason, too, they are sad, even when the kill lies at their feet. Best leave them alone till –

GREY BROTHER [*pointing*]: But how if men do not leave us alone? [*Sniffs.*] There is one afoot yonder.

[*The company verify the point one after another, stiffening to attention with a low whisper of Man! Man! Man! Mowgli lifts his head scowling.*]

MOWGLI: Here on my first night? [*Hand to mouth.*] And my mouth still bleeds. Akela! Bring me the head![5]

AKELA [*bounding forth*]: Hai! That is better! Good hunting!

MOWGLI: We must teach those stone-throwers their lesson. I'll roll the head to the village gates this very dawn. [*A pause.*]

BAGHEERA: What does Akela do? I have not heard[6] the death-cry.

GREY BROTHER: He is old, and a shade slow on the kill. Now I –
[*Enter* AKELA.]

AKELA: Must I bring in the head of the Little White One who called to thee from the village-wall?

MOWGLI: The Little White One! Seven times never! She must have the protection of the Jungle. [*Aside.*] What does Dulia here?

BAGHEERA [*aside*]: Bring me the head. Give her the protection of the Jungle. He turns quicker than a hunted buck. Oho! Truly man goes to man at the last.

WOLVES [*sullenly*]: What have we to do with man? Is not thy Jungle enough?

MOWGLI: Down! She is my kill! [*Motions with his hand as beasts drop out of sight.*]

DULIA [*without, singing*]:

Now I was born of woman kind and laid on a mother's breast,*

---

* This line echoes line 4 of 'The Only Son', the poem that prefaces 'In the Rukh' (*Many Inventions*): 'Now, was I born of womankind and laid in a mother's breast?' Otherwise, the lines are new.

But *he* lay out in the wet and the wind and the grey wolf guarded
   his rest.
Feet in the thicket and eyes in the dark[7] – lifters of cattle and kine –
   Lords of the wilderness, leave of your courtesy – the friends of my
   brother are mine.

[*Enters and stands surprised.*] I have walked in the fear of death
since I fled from death in the village. Here is the Rock. [MOWGLI
shows himself.] Mowgli!

MOWGLI: Here am I, Little White One – Dulia. [*Comes down from
the Council Rock.*] Have the man-pack cast thee out too?

DULIA [*panting*]: They have bound my mother and my father. They
   have taken our cattle, our grain, our cooking-pots. When the
   moon rises they will burn us alive. Help us! Oh, help us!

MOWGLI: They have bound Messua who was kind to me. [*Aside.*]
   Why? Oh I forgot.[8] They are men.

DULIA: She bade me follow and find thee if I could. My wrists are
   small [*holds them up*], so I slipped through the thongs. See?

MOWGLI: But they are torn and bleeding. *Men* did this – to thee
   . . . By the Bull that bought me, I will take a price for this! I will
   make an end of them and their cattle and their crops.

DULIA: Art thou mad? I ask thee for help, and thou canst only talk
   to the darkness. Come with me and help my folk, or they die –
   they die in the fire when the moon rises.

MOWGLI: I will come before moonrise,[9] and they shall not die in
   the fire. Run back, Little White One, and wait for me near the
   village. There is great hunting afoot.

DULIA [*making as to drag him forward*]: Nay, come thou now and save.

MOTHER WOLF: Will she drag him back to the man-pack, Bagheera?
   The wounds they dealt him are not yet dry.

BAGHEERA: That is the trail of men.[10] Having escaped one trap, they
   straightway hurry into another.

DULIA [*to* MOWGLI]: Ay, if ever thou hast loved our people, come
   with me.

MOWGLI [*to beasts*]: Wait a little. I – I must go with her. She is
   afraid.

WOLVES: Hear the Free Hunters, man-cub. Come back to thy Jungle. We know the man-pack. [*Crescendo as they rise one by one, showing themselves in semi-circle.*] Leave men alone.

BAGHEERA [*aside, crossing to* MOWGLI]: Ay, but this is not a man.

DULIA [*sinking into* MOWGLI's *arms as she sees the beasts*]: The Gods protect us! We are dead already.

MOWGLI [*his arm round her*]: Those! They are my people – therefore thy servants. Was my tale of the Rock a fairy tale? Nay, look up. I am the brother to wolves. [*Furiously to semi-circle as* DULIA *collapses.*] By whose leave do ye show yourselves, Free Hunters?

MOTHER WOLF: By whose leave dost thou take one of the man-pack into our Councils?

MOWGLI: By whose leave did I kill Shere Khan?[11]

MOTHER WOLF: Nay, do not be angry, my son. I bear the girl no ill-will, only thy trail and hers do not run together.

BAGHEERA: Of that I am not so sure.

MOWGLI [*over* DULIA]: The Red Flower burn your lairs, senseless[12] dogs! The girl is half dead with fear. Nay, look up, Dulia.

WOLVES: Let Baloo speak what is in our mouths.

BALOO: Man-cub, the Free Hunters are ill-pleased. The Rage of jealousy is on them. Bid the girl go.

MOWGLI: No. By the Bull that bought me, no!

MOTHER WOLF: What have we to do with men? This thing will take away from me my Lord and my cub whom I suckled. Let her go.

A WOLF: No. Make sure. The head! The head! The head! The head of the white thing that turns our brother's heart from his own people.

WOLVES [*together*]: The head! The head! The head!

AKELA [*stiffly crossing to* MOWGLI – *to* BAGHEERA]: I do not love men, but he saved my life at the Council Rock – Baloo?

BALOO [*crossing over and striking lightly with paw*]: I have spoken as the pack asked me, but I shall fight to please old Baloo.

[MOWGLI *still bends over* DULIA.]

DULIA (*sliding out of his arms, face in hands*): I fear! I am afraid! I would not look at my death.

[*Dead silence for ten seconds.* MOWGLI *raises his head, looks round the semi-circle, takes in the situation, rises to his feet, wraps cloak round left arm, draws knife, balances it and nods.*]

MOWGLI: I have said.

MOTHER WOLF: Nay – nay. We will not bare a tooth against *thee.* It is the girl!

MOWGLI [*settling himself in his tracks*]: She is my kill. I fight for my kill as I was taught in the pack. Who comes?

GREY BROTHER: Be wise, Brother. We will not even mouth that thing. Only bid it go away and trouble our Jungle no more.

BALOO AND AKELA: That is good talk – we say it, though we fight on thy side. Let us make an end of man in our Jungle.

[MOWGLI *draws a deep breath, drops point of knife and lowers left arm.*]

MOTHER WOLF [*pleadingly*]: What is one more kill more or less, my son? Come to the Jungle.

MOWGLI [*smiles and looks round – stoops to lay his hand on* DULIA*'s head. She sobs. He withdraws it and slides it round* BAGHEERA*'s neck.*] Black Cat of the Jungle, thou hast not spoken. Shall I give up this kill?

BAGHEERA: If I know man, this is something more than a kill. It is for the life.

MOWGLI [*dropping cloak and knife*]: Ay, the life.

[BAGHEERA *crouches behind him ready to spring, as he stands unarmed over* DULIA.]

WOLVES: The head! The head! The head! The Red Rage is on us! Kill!

MOWGLI [*arms folded*]: And who hinders?

MOTHER WOLF: Stand aside from the kill, then, my son.

MOWGLI: Didst thou give *me* up to Shere Khan when he sought *my* life?[13] [*Eyes pack as it gathers irresolute. Very slight and significant action (without music) on the part of* BALOO *and* AKELA. BAGHEERA *head between paws slightly raises head.*] My people are very strong. [*Points to* DULIA.] They have frightened one weak thing here senseless. My people are very brave. They fear she will turn my heart from the jungle. My people are very wise. They will slay her that I may love them better. O strong, brave and wise, hear

50

me – weak, unarmed and simple – [*All this with deep scorn.*] I will
not give up my kill, nor my right to kill, and I will not take orders
from any pack under the stars because I am a man and ye are
wolves. Kill as ye choose, but if ye kill one ye must kill both.
Shall I cry our death-cry? [*Throws back hair, raises hand, as in
scene over* SHERE KHAN*'s body.*] For the kill – the double kill –
Full gorge! Full gorge! It is met! It is met! It is met!

[*A long pause. Pack get together and confer.*]

BALOO [*amazed*]: He pulls the very whiskers of Death. What will
he do, Bagheera?

BAGHEERA: I know somewhat of man's cunning, but this trail is hid
from me.

MOWGLI: What, are ye all full fed? Here is my throat, Grey Brother.
It has lain often enough under thy muzzle in the lair. Spring and
make an end.

GREY BROTHER: Not I – Little Brother, not I – my Lord.

MOWGLI [*merrily*]: Must I hawk my carcass up and down the Jungle
all night? Ah, yonder is one that has always hated man. There is
no drop of her milk in my blood. *She* will not flinch and cower.
[MOTHER WOLF *drops, cowering.*] Lair-Mother! Here is my heart.
[*Half choking.*] It has beat against thine all through the cold nights
when I was a cub. [*Gesture.*] Tear it out, Mother.

MOTHER WOLF: Nay – nay. Be silent, cub of my suckling. Thy
words sting like the Red Flower. I – I am thy Lair-Mother.[14]

MOWGLI: Huh! It was not *I* that forgot that. [*Changes manner to
most winning tenderness. Steps clear of* DULIA, *drops on one knee and
holds out arms.*] Wolves of the pack – Free Hunters – my brothers![15]

WOLVES [*penitently*]: We are shamed – shamed – shamed. We will
hunt at thy bidding. We are thy people – we are thy dogs. Do
not mock us any more, my Lord.

MOWGLI [*kneeling*]: Nay, but I love ye. [*Arm over* LAIR-MOTHER.]
Indeed I love ye better because ye hated me a little even now.

BAGHEERA: Hated him a little. I never looked to see one bone of
him next[16] the other after he dropt his knife. [*Half rising; seriously.*]
So then Free Hunters – bastards of Tabaqui – is this trail ended,
or must I –

MOWGLI: Peace, Black Cat. My brothers and I have spoken to me and my brothers. The trail is only beginning – a new and terrible trail. I go to make an end of man. [*Stoops above* DULIA.]

BAGHEERA: Is that the way to get about it? [*Grumbling.*] Peace, Black Cat, forsooth – as though I were one of the Monkey People . . . But he is a man – a man. [*Grumble dies down.*]

MOWGLI: See what ye have done! [*To* DULIA.] Nay, look up. It is not death. My people come to do thee honour. [*Half raising her.*] Those very friends for whom I took Shere Khan's hide. Those very friends whose eyes thou wast so keen to scratch yesterday. Do not tremble. They are mine and thine.[17] [*Lays her head on his shoulder.*] Look! [*To beasts.*] Be humble! Your eyes on the earth and your heads at her feet. If ye frighten her again –

WOLVES: Nay – we are thy dogs and hers.

DULIA [*opening her eyes. Half held by* MOWGLI *in rapt voice*]: These are they whom we fear by night and by day. The wolf – the grey wolf – the panther of the cattle-pen – and the bear that is as wise as a man . . . and I stand among them and they harm me not . . . and thou [*amazement and realization in her eyes*]. Thou art their Lord.

MOWGLI [*laughing*]: Yes. That has been made certain – I am also their brother.

DULIA [*recovering, standing away from* MOWGLI]: Then why should I fear?

MOWGLI [*admiring as she touches* BAGHEERA*'s neck*]: Oh, well spoken, Little White One. What can Buldeo and his priests do against these?

DULIA [*clasping hands agitatedly*]: Oh, my father and mother! I have forgotten them.

MOWGLI: I have not. Go back, Little White One, through the Jungle – which is *thy* Jungle,[18] and tell them that not a hair of their heads shall be touched. I will come before the moon rises with these [*points to beasts*], and I will take a price from the village[19] [*picks up her hands*],[20] the price of the blood on these hands . . . Dost thou believe?

DULIA: I believe. My Lord, I believe.[21] [*Exit.*]

MOWGLI [*over shoulder curtly to wolves*]: Grey Brother, bid Hathi the Elephant come hither.[22]

GREY BROTHER: Little Brother, indeed and truly I – thou – we cannot bid Hathi come and go as though he were a deer. He is a Lord of Life and Death.

MOWGLI [*with restrained passion*]: And I am something of the same breed, and master of the Red Flower to boot. I have been crossed enough to-night. Hear me once for all. It is not Mowgli the wolf-cub who speaks. It is a man who goes to make an end of man. [*Exit* GREY BROTHER. MOWGLI *takes stage, scowling*.] Now, Hathi shall help me in my war against the man-pack.[23] By *her* blood on my hands, I will have no truce with them[24] . . . [*Strikes with knife*.] What is a mere killing beside this that they have done to *her*?[25] Buldeo – the priests – the men[26] that threw stones [*raises hand to mouth*], all who saw it and all who suffered it. I will make an end of all – all.

MOTHER WOLF [*to* BAGHEERA]: This is not the man-cub I suckled. It is a new Mowgli and I fear.

BALOO: I taught him the Law, but I – even I – am afraid. What will he do, Bagheera? Is he wrath against any of us? Speak to him.

BAGHEERA: Not I. He outfaced the pack when they were mad with the Red Rage of Jealousy. I am Bagheera, but even I will not cross his trail now.[27]

AKELA: And yet he was not wrath when the man-pack cast him out. He came back to us openly glad.

BAGHEERA: And then came that Little White One, wounded. Akela, hast thou never fought for thy mate in thy time?

AKELA: Oho! Does the trail run *that* way? It will be *very*[28] good hunting.

[*All this time* MOWGLI *scowls and meditates, digging into the turf with his knife*.]

MOWGLI: Is Hathi here?

HATHI [*head and shoulders only visible in the high grass*]: Good hunting, my Lord!

[BAGHEERA *comes forward and crouches at* MOWGLI's *feet*.]

53

MOWGLI: Good hunting, silent one. It was told me when I was with the man-pack [*spits*] that thou wast trapped by man?

HATHI: Once I fell into a pit. A sharp stake in it scarred me from heel to shoulder. I carry the mark still.

MOWGLI: Then didst thou go away?

HATHI: Till my wound healed.

MOWGLI: And then?

HATHI: Then I strode back to the fields of those men who trapped me.

MOWGLI: When?

HATHI: When their crops were ready to reap.

MOWGLI: Who reaped those crops?

HATHI: I and my three sons, trumpeting by night.

MOWGLI: Who ploughed after ye had reaped?

HATHI: There were none to plough. I and my three sons broke in the huts of the villagers. They[29] ran away.

MOWGLI: Where are those villages?

HATHI: The Jungle has covered them. Go far as a man can walk between sunset and dawn, none can say: – 'Here stood my house', or 'Here did I plough', or 'Here did I pray to my Gods'.

MOWGLI: It was well done, Hathi with the scar, but a second time it shall be better done, because there is a man to direct.

BAGHEERA: Woe! Woe! To the man-pack. A great fear comes by this trail!

MOWGLI: Ye know the village of the man-pack that cast me out. They are senseless and cruel. They do not kill for food, they kill for sport. When they are idle, they throw their own bread into the Red Flower. It is not good they should live here any more.

HATHI: Kill then –

MOWGLI: What good are dry bones to me? Look! Here is Shere Khan's hide, but Shere Khan is not in it, and [*gesture of empty hand flung forward*] I do not know where he is gone. This time I will have what I can see and touch. [*Stabs into grass with knife.*] When the moon rises I go down with these my servants,[30] and I drive the man-pack out of the lairs where they lie down and the streets where they walk. There shall not remain in that village

ACT III. SCENE I

by midnight one thing[31] that scoops water with its hands or eats food burned over the Red Flower.[32] That shall be my work, but lest they return again to their lairs, let in the Jungle upon that village, Hathi![33]

BAGHEERA: I never feared man yet – but now I fear.

WOLVES:[34] Wah! Man lets in the Jungle upon man!

MOWGLI:[35] Lest[36] they return again, upon their fields and their houses and their temples and their water-tanks,[37] let in the Jungle, Hathi!

HATHI: But I – but we have no quarrel with them. Must we kill? My tusks have been red once. I would not wake that smell again.

MOWGLI: Nor I. But they have trapped a woman who called me her son . . . I have seen . . . I have smelled the blood of one who called me brother in the man-pack. She did them no harm, but they have torn and wounded her. Only the smell of the Jungle grass on their doorsteps can take away that taint.[38] Let in the Jungle, Hathi!

HATHI: So did the scar on my hide burn till I watched the fields hidden by the Jungle grass. Thy war shall be our war. We will open their roofs to the sun; we will trample their walls to the earth. We will let in the Jungle. [*Trumpets.*]

MOWGLI [*to beasts*]: Ye have heard? We will go down and drive out. Behind us Hathi and his sons will destroy. Is it good hunting?

AKELA: Wilt thou not now let me take Buldeo's head?

MOWGLI: Never! It is the blood of a man – it burns like the Red Flower. Let *them* spill it if they choose, but they must do it far off. Up! Free Hunters under the moon! For the man-pack that burns and slays and says the thing that is not – that traps and wounds women,[39] bitter, stupid, unclean – it is met! Oh, it is met! It is met! Who follows the man-cub?

BAGHEERA: Man-cub no more. Who dare disobey the Lord of the Jungle? Hail to the Lord of the Waste!

OMNES: Hail to the Lord of the Waste!

SCENE 2

Outside MESSUA's *hut.* MESSUA *and* RAWAL *bound on cots. Torches and murmur of* VOICES *behind the barred door of courtyard.*

VOICES [*intoning without*]: Hear us, Gods of the Homestead. Merciful Godlings of the village, accept the sacrifice. We have taken the evil-doers, them that deal with magicians, sorcerers and wizards. By fire shall their wicked hearts be cleansed. Hear us, oh Gods of the Homestead, till the sacrifice is accepted, for we are afraid – afraid – afraid!

RAWAL: And this comes of being charitable to wizards.

MESSUA: No! Though they burn me for it, Mowgli is no sorcerer ... And Dulia[40] may bring help. At least she is safe from the fire!

RAWAL: Safe? In the Jungle by night?[41] Well, better be slain by beasts than men. They have taken my cattle, my grain, our cooking-pots, and thy ornaments ... and when the moon rises they will kill us.

MESSUA: We are in the hands of the Gods. But Mowgli was never a sorcerer. He was like my boy Nathoo, bold, saucy and fearless ... and Dulia is safe ... from the fire.

DULIA [*entering boldly*]: Mother! I have seen him among his people. He will come and do justice.

MESSUA: My daughter! Speak low and hide. The village may hear thee.

DULIA [*with gesture of contempt*]: What do I care for the village – *now*! I have seen what I have seen. The Jungle is alive and awake. Eyes that glare behind bushes: feet that walk in the darkness are about us, and he – he – is Lord of them all.

RAWAL: She is mad with fear! Hide thee, my daughter.

[DULIA *poses in an attitude of healthy contempt; laughing a little. Enter* MOWGLI *and stoops over* MESSUA, *cutting thongs with a jerk.*]

MOWGLI: Faugh! What jackal's work is this?

MESSUA: I knew – I knew thou wouldst help me, my son. [*Embraces him.*]

MOWGLI: Nay, not yet; I am too new from the Jungle. [*Cuts* RAWAL*'s bands.*] By the Bull that bought me! Why – *why* – have the man-pack done this?

RAWAL [*sitting up stiffly*]: Because we made a son of thee. Look, I bleed!

MOWGLI: Oh, thou art a man. Wipe it off. [*Turns scornfully.* MESSUA *lays a hand timidly on his arm.*]

MESSUA: I gave thee food and drink because thou wast like my son Nathoo. I loved thee . . . and Buldeo and the others said thou wast a devil in league with beasts, and therefore those who loved thee must die.

MOWGLI [*to* DULIA]: Thou didst not tell me this. [*Tenderly.*] And thou wast bound too. [*To* MESSUA.] What is a devil? Death and my beasts I know.

MESSUA [*hysterically*]: See, I said he was no sorcerer. He speaks as my boy would have spoken.

RAWAL: What good is that to us? Sorcerer or no sorcerer, we be dead already.

MOWGLI: Why? Hands and feet are free. [*Points off.*] There is the road.

RAWAL [*pointing over wall*]: They would follow us and drag us here again.

MOWGLI: When the moon rises, they will have other work to do.

DULIA: My father, he speaks truth. We are safe from all harm.

RAWAL [*scornfully*]: Safe – in the Jungle – by night? [*Thoughtfully.*] Well! At least beasts do not rob. If there is a chance. [*Stands and digs furiously with hands under eave of cottage.*]

MOWGLI: Neither man nor beast will slay you. There will be a watch about you. [*To* DULIA.] Thou knowest?

DULIA: I know, my Lord. I have seen what I have seen.

MOWGLI [*to* MESSUA, *pointing to* RAWAL]: He will be afraid, but thou wilt believe.

MESSUA: Ay, my son. Man, ghost, or wolf of the Jungle, I believe.

RAWAL [*still digging*]: We must get to Kanhiwara, where the English live –

MOWGLI [*pointing down*]: But *that* is not the way.

MESSUA [*half ashamed*]: It is his little money he has hidden.

MOWGLI: Oh, the stuff that goes from hand to hand, and never gets any warmer. Do they use it at Kanhiwara too?

RAWAL [*scornfully*]: To speak thus of good silver! Huh! *He* is no sorcerer. Let us haste. [*Slipping money into bosom.*] I can buy help on the road with this –

MOWGLI: Those who help thee to-night do not use – money.

RAWAL [*looking round vengefully; sinking voice*]: If I reach Kanhiwara alive, I will have justice for my cattle, my grain and my cooking-pots.[42]

MOWGLI: I have never met justice but – come next rains and see what is left.

MESSUA [*horrified*]: Dost thou stay here?

MOWGLI [*with an unpleasant smile*]: Surely. It is my village, where I feast all my friends.

MESSUA: They will kill thee.

MOWGLI [*to* DULIA]: Thou hast seen my friends. Will they?

DULIA [*laughs*]: I do not think any man will touch my Lord.

RAWAL: Oh! They are both mad. [*Wolf howls off. He starts back.*] And the Jungle is full of beasts.

MOWGLI [*over his shoulder, facing toward* DULIA, *with a little laugh*]: Oh, but I forget. There may be some singing and talking about your road to-night. It is the protection of the Jungle.

RAWAL: Singing and talking! If ever I heard a dog-wolf give tongue . . . [*Stands irresolute fingering long staff.*]

MOWGLI: Come then, next rains, Little White One, and I will show thee a new village – when I have cleansed this one.

DULIA: I owe my life to my Lord. I have seen what I have seen. Surely I will come. [*Holds out hand.*]

MESSUA [*to* RAWAL *who is shrinking*]: I will lead. I do not know his powers but he speaks as a king. Come Dulia.

MOWGLI [*taking her hand, sees blood on her wrist and scowls. Then softly*]: A new village, full of flowers and fruit for us to play in.

DULIA: I am only a girl – my Lord is Lord of the Jungle . . . How can we play together any more?

MOWGLI [*easily and interestedly*]: Why is that? It is true I am brother

58

to wolves and Lord of Life and Death in the Jungle, but still I
am Mowgli and thou art Dulia my playmate.

DULIA [*overwhelmed*]: If my Lord wills, who am I to –

[*Throughout this dialogue* MESSUA *looks at the young couple with
appropriate expression.* RAWAL *shuffles off.*]

RAWAL: Haste! The priests will be here in a moment . . .

MOWGLI [*with scorn*]: They? Oh, I had forgotten them. Farewell
then – and do not look back!

[*Exeunt* MESSUA, RAWAL *and* DULIA. *A wolf howls off. Confused
murmur behind courtyard wall.*]

VOICES: They are safe enough. Wait till the moon rises. It's unlucky
to kill witches in the dark. Heat the gun-barrels, Buldeo.

MOWGLI [*scornfully, listening*]: Ah, Buldeo – that great hunter,
Buldeo. [*Enter* MOTHER WOLF.] What is it, Lair-Mother?

MOTHER WOLF: I have seen the woman who calls thee her son.
Bagheera spoke truth: man goes to man at last.

MOWGLI: May be – but to-night I am very far from that trail . . .
Follow them and let all the Jungle know they are safe.

MOTHER WOLF: I obey. Do not forget that I was thy Lair-Mother
in the cave long ago, and there is wolf's milk in thy blood.

MOWGLI [*taking stage*]: It is more like the Red Flower. Why do the
man-pack not begin? [*Listening.*] Oh, we must wait till moonrise,
must we. Pah! I would not torture even Tabaqui thus . . . Is it
wolf's milk or man's milk that holds me from tearing them all to
pieces? [*Enter* BAGHEERA.]

MOWGLI [*curtly*]: Has Hathi come down from the hills?

BAGHEERA: He is at the far gate with Baloo. Akela and the pack lie
under the walls. We all wait thy word. By the lock that freed me
this will be good hunting! What shall I do? When I do not follow
a certain man-cub whom I love, they call me a Lord of Life and
Death in the Jungle. Shall I sing to thy man-pack? Shall I dance
for their children?

MOWGLI: At thy pleasure, old hunter. I have no stomach for jesting
till I have driven them out – out – out!

BAGHEERA [*aside*]: This is the man-cub I do not know. [*Aloud.*] Forgive me; I am but a black panther and thou art Lord of the Jungle.

I will go humbly. Yes, I will be a cat – a village cat. [*Sees cot and leaps up.*] Will the man-pack caress me, think you? Oh, hairless ones – eaters of earth – I am Bagheera – in the night, and my strength is in me. Who comes to play with Bagheera – the strayed cat?

MOWGLI: The moon rises. I must oversee the drive – [*turns towards hut hesitatingly*] – or the kill.

BAGHEERA: Have a care! Less than a hair would turn this jest to a red killing. Our people are half mad already with the smell of man. *Thou* must hold them.

MOWGLI: Well I know it. But who will hold Mowgli? [*Climbs roof of hut and stands silhouetted against moon as it rises. Gate opens to clamour and flicker of torches.*]

VOICES [*intoning*]: Accept the sacrifice, Gods of the Homestead. Oh known and comfortable Godlings of birth and death and marriage, of ploughing and sowing and reaping and harvest, accept the sacrifice. Take the lives of the evil-doers that have trafficked with devils, and give us plenty. Bless the cattle and the crops and the little children, that we may be peaceful and rich from this day forward.

BULDEO [*shouts*]: Now we are come to punish the sorcerers!

MOWGLI [*from roof*]: What, again, Buldeo?

BULDEO [*as he throws open door*]: The Jungle-devil himself! Bind and slay. Wait till I get my gun.

MOWGLI [*hand raised to check* BAGHEERA *who crouches unseen on cot*]: By thy permission this is my hunting to-night, Buldeo. [*Drops hand;* BAGHEERA *surges forward with one long aaah! General scatter and hurroosh.* Yells of 'Panther! a black panther!'*]

MOWGLI [*on roof, hands to mouth*]: Let go! The drive! The drive! E-eea! – Lu! Lu! Lu! Lu! Out! – Drive out!

[*Fresh rush of people and yells of 'A wolf! a wolf! Wolf in the temple! – Sorcery! Sorcery! The Jungle is upon us! Whither shall we fly?' A wolf shows against the roof of a hut. There is a general howling and then a silence.*]

---

* The typescript reads 'scatted and hurrust'. 'Hurroosh', meaning 'a tremendous fuss or uproar' (Partridge, *Dictionary of Slang*), occurs a few lines later in this scene.

MOWGLI: Out! Drive out! What is it? [*Stamps foot.*]

AKELA [*from a housetop*]: They have gone to eeearth! [*Long whoop.*]
Shall we dig them out?

CRIES: Shut the doors! Bring in the children! Bar the gates!

MOWGLI: Hathi! [*Trumpet of an elephant.*] Break down the roofs
above them. Herd them out into the street . . . Out, drive out!

A WOLF: They throw stones here. May we kill?

MOWGLI: No. Drive with a shut mouth. Out! Out, man-pack!

[*A crash and* HATHI's *head is seen above falling timber. Fresh
howls and hurrooshes from the crowd. They surge into courtyard and
huddle together.*]

MOWGLI [*with uplifted hands; war-dance against the moon*]: I will let
loose against you the fleet-footed vine in the gates of these your
councils . . .*

VOICES: The sorcerer! The sorcerer! Our Gods have forsaken us!
Fly! Fly! Do not wait to gather anything.

[*Crowd thins out with rattle of feet retiring and murmur of voices. A
long silence. One wolf howls far off.*]

AKELA: Gone away! Gone away! Back, Free Hunters under the
moon!

MOWGLI: Is it finished?

BALOO: Empty as an old bee-comb.

---

* From 'Mowgli's Song Against People', following 'Letting in the Jungle' in *The
Second Jungle Book*. The quotation conflates the first line of the first stanza and part
of the first line of the second stanza of the poem. The two stanzas read thus:

> I will let loose against you the fleet-footed vines –
> I will call in the Jungle to stamp out your lines!
> > The roofs shall fade before it,
> > > The house-beams shall fall;
> > And the *Karela*, the bitter *Karela*,
> > > Shall cover it all!

> In the gates of these your councils my people shall sing.
> In the doors of these your garners the Bat-folk shall cling;
> > And the snake shall be your watchman,
> > > By a hearthstone unswept;
> > For the *Karela*, the bitter *Karela*,
> > > Shall fruit where ye slept!

BAGHEERA [*turning with upraised paw*]: Empty as a bullock's skull.

HATHI [*head and shoulders showing*]: The hearths are cold; the roofs are broken; the streets are silent. I have let in the Jungle.

MOWGLI: And the hearths shall be cold, and the roofs shall be broken and the streets shall be silent for ever – even till with my own hands I feed the fires again and with my own tongue bid the man-pack return. I take the trees and the wind and the rain to witness that this is my village. Cleanse it for me, oh wind and rain. Cover it again, oh trees and Jungle grass, for here is my lair!

ACT IV

SCENE I

The village overgrown by Jungle. MOWGLI *lying in hammock of creepers opposite the temple. Red painted Hindu God partly visible through creepers and flowers.* BAGHEERA *and* BALOO *asleep, right and left under hammock.*

MOWGLI [*yawning and stretching himself*]: Is it time to hunt yet, Black Cat of my village?

BAGHEERA: Not yet. Lie still and be glad. The year has turned – the grass grows again; the sun is warmer day by day; the time of New Talk begins.

MOWGLI: What is the time of New Talk to me? I am *not* glad. I am most sorrowful. [*Pushes him with foot.*] Wake up and be sorrowful with me.

BAGHEERA: Who can be sorrowful when the time of New Talk is so near?

BALOO: Is thy nose hot? Are thy ears cold? Run and eat a little grass.

MOWGLI: The Red Flower lick up all the grass in the Jungle. I think I have eaten poison. Sometimes I am hot when it is cold. Then I am cold when it is warm. The air is soft, but I tingle all over as though it stung me . . . I lie down, but I do not sleep.

BALOO: Thou hast eaten too much meat. Roots and honey are best for the blood when the year turns.

MOWGLI: I bathe and I am not made cool. I laugh but I do not

63

rejoice. I hear footsteps following me. I turn and there is no one. I look behind the trees. There is no one.

BAGHEERA: How should there be? We have swept the village clean.

MOWGLI: I know, but still I listen. Then I run back and forth, calling, calling.

BAGHEERA: For whom?

MOWGLI: I cannot tell – I cannot tell. I ache from head to heel: my bones are like water and my eyes are as heavy as my heart. *Is* it poison, think you?

BAGHEERA [*aside*]: The time of the New Talk works on him at last. [*Aloud, with intention.*] Baloo what poison may our Lord have eaten?

BALOO: In the time of the New Talk that poison is in the air.

MOWGLI: Ye both mock me. I will ask Hathi the Elephant; he is very wise.

BAGHEERA: Better ask Pherao, the scarlet woodpecker. He is still wiser. [*Half rising.*] By the Lock that freed me, yonder he goes! Welcome! Welcome! Red-Head. What word of the time of New Talk? We are waiting.

PHERAO [*off, music*]: Close, close at hand, Bagheera. [*Sings.*]

> With the faithful sun and the fruitful cloud
> Northward my flight I wing.
> News! News! News!
> Bird in the thicket and buck on the plain
> Lords of the Jungle riot again,
> I give you the leave of the spring!

MOWGLI: Now in all my life, I have never heard Pherao sing thus.

BALOO: And yet he has sung thus seventeen times since thou wast a cub, and seventeen times I have forgotten I was a Lord of Life and Death in the Jungle, and have gone rioting forth like a cub of the second year.

MOWGLI [*haughtily*]: I am not a cub, and that noise only makes me seventy times more sorrowful. It is a senseless song; it runs in the head like a grasshopper's chirp when one would sleep.

BAGHEERA: Dost thou wish to sleep? Hark!

ACT IV. SCENE I

[*Music off, as the Jungle wakes.*]

For our white and our excellent nights: for our nights of swift
    running.
    Fair ranging, far seeing: good hunting: sure cunning!
For the smells of the dawning, untainted ere dew has departed!
For the cry of our mates through the dark and the answer
    hot-hearted!
    For the risk and the riot of night!
    For the sleep at the lair-mouth by day –
      It is met and we haste to delight!
        Bay! O Bay!*

MOWGLI: Are we all his jackals that we must shout when that
red-headed gipsy gives tongue?

BAGHEERA [*aside*]: When Pherao sings we are all his jackals. [*Aloud, mocking.*] And [how?] is it with thee, Lord of the Jungle?

MOWGLI: Again the hot and cold fits. I must sweat it out in the
hunt. [*Calls off.*] Oh brothers, who hunts with the Lord of the
Jungle?

BAGHEERA: Very few this night, I think. [*Exit.*]

    [BALOO *crouches and hides.*]

---

* Untitled verses at the head of 'Red Dog' (*The Second Jungle Book*), considerably altered. In their original form they read thus:

For our white and our excellent nights – for the nights of swift running,
    Fair ranging, far-seeing, good hunting, sure cunning!
For the smells of the dawning, untainted, ere dew has departed!
For the rush through the mist, and the quarry blind-started!
For the cry of our mates when the sambhur has wheeled and is standing at
    bay
    For the risk and the riot of night!
    For the sleep at the lair-mouth by day.
      It is met, and we go to the fight.
        Bay! O Bay!

PHERAO [*off*]:

> She has stirred the sap of the oldest tree
>> And the young buds yearn to her dew –
> She has broken the bonds of the jealous year –
>> That the timid peoples forget their fear.
> Lords of the Jungle, hear, oh hear!
>> Go to your mates anew.

MOWGLI: Are they all deaf? I am sick – sick, Bagheera. I will hunt alone. No. I do not care to kill. I am sick – sick. Dost thou hear me, Black Cat? [*Looks round.*] Bagheera gone too, and I do not see Baloo. They would never have left me except they knew that I must die. Yes. That is it. That is the meaning of these flushes and pains and aches and emptiness. Doubtless I have eaten poison and Death will come for me. [*Sits down; takes off knife and wreath.*] The very smell of these flowers troubles me. Oh, what is it? What is it?

BALOO: What dost thou do?

MOWGLI [*severely*]: Being forsaken by all my friends, and mocked by all the Jungle – even the trees mock me – and moreover being troubled by a new and terrible sickness for which thou hast mocked me, I wait for Death.

BALOO [*aside*]: By the Law I taught him, he takes my jest for truth! [*Aloud.*] All in good time.

DULIA [*far off*]: Mowgli!

BALOO [*listens, head on one side, with absurd gravity*]: One calls thee by name. Perhaps it is Death.

MOWGLI: I did not know he comes for men thus, but I am ready. [*Calls in tense attitude.*] I am here, O Death! [*Aside.*] It will be a great fight. Stay and watch, Baloo. I may slay him.

DULIA [*without*]: Mowgli! Oh, Mowgli!

BALOO: Shall I watch this fight?

MOWGLI [*wrathfully, but half laughing*]: *That* Death! It is the Little White One . . . Baloo, I will pull out all thy whiskers for this. [*Listens and looks off.*]

BALOO: Who said it was Death? Not I. Good hunting, most wise Lord of the Jungle. [*Exit.*]

DULIA: My Lord is lord of the Lord of the Night –
            Of the hunters that walk in the shade.
            I hear them about me to left and to right;
            Why should his slave be afraid?

[*Enters.*] Oh, Mowgli! [*Rushes forward to embrace him. Recoils and bows to his feet.*] My Lord!

MOWGLI [*at gaze, entranced*]: It is Dulia! Nay, look at me! None look at me between the eyes in the Jungle. Look at me!

                    [DULIA *looks, half dropping veil.*]

MOWGLI: What is it? [*Covers face with hand.*] My eyes dazzle – and thine are like stars.

DULIA [*recovering upper hand – woman-fashion*]: Not a word of greeting, my Lord?

MOWGLI [*staring abstractedly, then shaking himself into recollection*]: I had forgotten. Be welcome, Little White One. Here is our new village – full of flowers, as I said: but the fruit is not yet ripe. [*Stoops to pick up wreath, and crowns her.*] Will these flowers suffice? I – I have nothing else to give. I – I am alone, as thou seest.

DULIA: I see. [*Looks round and shivers.*] And thou hast lived here alone since we parted.

MOWGLI: Assuredly – with my people. And thou?

DULIA: I have lived at Kanhiwara with my people.

MOWGLI: The Kanhiwara man-pack have not cast thee out, then?

DULIA: No: but I – but we wished to see the old fields again. They are very dear to us.

MOWGLI: The Jungle has swallowed them.

DULIA: My father said we should be slain by beasts, but my mother said that thy people would never harm one of us. So we came.

MOWGLI: But what didst thou say? Ah, it is good to hear thee speak again.

DULIA: I said to my father and mother: – 'Wait by the river, and I will go forward alone and lay my petition before the Lord of the Jungle.' [*Sinks on one knee with clasped hands.*] Will he hear me?

MOWGLI [*aside*]: Hear her! It is the voice I have listened for since spring came. [*Aloud.*] I hear.

DULIA [*pathetic stop open*]: We played together in the village. The streets are empty now.

MOWGLI: I emptied them.

DULIA: The roofs are broken that covered the homes of our delight and our labour.

MOWGLI: I spoke and Hathi broke them open to the sun.

DULIA: I lit the house-fires with fuel of thy bringing. The fires are cold now.

MOWGLI: I stamped out all the fires. It was the price of blood on these little hands. [*Takes them tenderly.*] I did well. [*Looks at her. His eyes fall. Covers his face again with a hand.*] Did I well?

DULIA: Do silent streets, broken roofs and cold hearth-stones please thee? Is it good to go wet with the dew, and lie houseless under the stars?

MOWGLI: It – was good.

DULIA [*half mocking*]: Good to hear no voice from dawn to dusk? To lie awake of nights listening for that voice? To dream of that voice at thy ear? To put out thy arms and to gather the darkness to thy heart? Is it good?

MOWGLI: But – but how dost thou know? This has been my sorrow, I think, for many days.

DULIA: And mine, I know, for many more.

MOWGLI [*intently*]: Did any tell you it was poison?

DULIA [*half veiling*]: I told no one, my Lord. I came to thee.

MOWGLI: Alas! How can I help? Yesterday I was Lord of the Jungle. To-day the very trees mock me.

DULIA: Ah, I have been mocked also.

MOWGLI: By my people? [*Angrily with furious gesture.*] I will –

DULIA: Nay, at Kanhiwara, by maidens of my years. [*Lays hand on arm.*]

MOWGLI: Wherefore?

DULIA [*slowly*]: Why did the Jungle mock thee, my Lord?

MOWGLI: I do not know, but I think it is because I have [   ]*

DULIA [*more slowly*]: So it was with the maidens.

---

* There is a gap of two lines' space here in the typescript.

MOWGLI: Then let us send and ask one of them.

DULIA [*petulantly*]: The Gods forbid. I did not come here to bring all the maids of Kanhiwara to guess riddles. I came to speak with thee – to beg a gift. Will my Lord give me his commands? Shall I return to my folk yonder [*points*], and tell them that the village is shut to me, or shall I bid them come in and roof the houses and light the house-fires?

MOWGLI [*recovering*]: I have no fire.

DULIA [*producing fire-pot*]: I have. No woman goes without it – even the fire that warms, cherishes and makes clean. [*Stands waiting, fire-pot in hand. A long pause.* PHERAO *is heard singing off.*]

MOWGLI: Light the fire.

[DULIA *goes to slab before Hindu idol, gathers a handful of dry rubbish on the cornice. Music off; soft.*]

DULIA: Yes, before the Gods. [*Busies herself with lighting fire.*]

MOWGLI [*watching her devouringly*]: How many, many rains since we last met?

DULIA: Only a year as men count time, but we women reckon otherwise. Will my Lord bring fuel?

MOWGLI: I am not thy Lord – I am thy servant.

DULIA: Be it so. [*Smiling.*] Mowgli, feed the fire. [*Picks up sticks and hands to him.* DULIA *sings.*]

> Ashes of fire at even,
>   Smoke to the timeless sky:
> And we mourn and we strive,
> And we woo and we wive
>   But the village endureth for aye.
>
> Gods of the garth* and the homestead,
>   Gods of the field and the byre;
> Grant us the hope of our toiling,
>   Love by the light of our fire!

---

* The typescript reads 'mark'. In the first appearance of the poem (see beginning of Act I, Scene 2), Kipling first wrote 'work' here, then altered it to 'garth'.

Ah, now it is alight. It shall all come back. The fire – the roofs above the fire, and presently little children about the hearth, leaping and falling and crying. [*As she sings and the fire blazes,* BAGHEERA, BALOO *and the* WOLVES *appear through the Jungle, but check at the motion of* MOWGLI's *hand.*] My people will see the flame through the trees and know.

MOWGLI: My people know already. Look! [DULIA *turns.*] Do not be afraid. They will not cast thee into the fire.

DULIA: Why should I fear? I owe them my life already. [*Stands up and holds out arms.*] Be welcome, masters of the Jungle!

BAGHEERA: By the Lock that freed me, this is a fit mate for the Lord of the Jungle.

BALOO: I hear the feet of the cubs – strong cubs – wrestling and tumbling down the glades. [*To* MOWGLI.] But I do not see Death here.

MOTHER WOLF [*with intention*]: I am too old for the time of New Talk. What of to-night's hunting, my son?

AKELA: Nay, Mother Wolf, he has killed already – a doe that came across the ranges to find him.

BAGHEERA: Eea! He is poisoned. [*To* MOWGLI.] Do thy bones still ache? Dost thou still listen for footfalls and voices? Shall we call Hathi to cure thee? He is very wise.

MOWGLI [*looking from voice to voice – hand raised half pleadingly*]: My brothers – wise ones. Never before in all my years in the Jungle –

BALOO: In all his years! Oh, hear him!

BAGHEERA [*very sarcastic*]: This is a new trail which our Lord will show to us. Lord of the Jungle – Head Wolf – Mowgli – [*melting*] beloved. Thy servants wait on thy wisdom. Never before in all thy years – eh?

MOWGLI [*rallying with a laugh*]: Thou hast sprung too soon for once in thy life, old hunter. Hear me! There was once in the Jungle an old Black Cat – whose coat [*stoops*] came away in mangy brown patches.

BAGHEERA [*indignantly*]: Mangy, indeed! Thou knowest a new sleek coat will grow before summer, manling.

BALOO: Nay, the word is with him, Bagheera. Thou art fairly trapped.

MOWGLI: And this Black Cat, evil and silent, lay still and purred with mirth when his Lord was troubled at the time of the New Talk, because of a secret which the Black Cat knew and would not tell. Yea, he mocked his Lord's wisdom; he did not attend his Lord's hunting call, and he made a jest of a sickness that overtook his Lord. A most bad Black Cat! But Baloo, who teaches the Law, was not a hair better, or Akela, nor anyone in the Jungle. They too knew the secret but they did not tell.

BAGHEERA [*looking at* BALOO]: Aha! Who is trapped now, my brothers?

BALOO: I trapped indeed! Pherao shouted that secret aloud through the Jungle! We heard, but Mowgli could not hear.

MOWGLI: Think ye? Then came to me, Mowgli the man, his Little White One – alone, and – [*Throws up hand.*] There is word for me also.

> He that soweth the streams in the sea,
>> And reapeth clouds from the deep,
> He that upholdeth the joy of the sky
> He hath not forgotten – he doth not deny
>> Man and maid,
>> Maid and man,
>> He sends them a secret to keep.
>
> He saith: – 'I have given my blessing to each
>> In the waters, the plain and the grove.
> The glory of life, the delight and the pride
> I have not forgotten, I have not denied
>> But to man
>> Maid and man –
>> To man I have given love!
> As it was in Eden when the four great rivers ran
> And I filled my earth with splendour for a maiden and a man
> When they saw that each was godlike and they knew what they
>> knew –

As it was in Eden, be it unto you!'

DULIA: Yes, it is surely the voice of the Gods.

MOWGLI: The Gods – ah! Good hunting, my brothers. [*Gesture of greeting towards the sky.*]

DULIA: Nay, the Gods are far above us – very mighty.

MOWGLI: Nay. They must be my brothers. Else why have they made me so joyful? [*To beasts.*] Did *ye* hear, my brothers?

BAGHEERA: It is too high for us. Our trails divide here.

BALOO: Never! We love him. Man goes to man at the last, but we will not cast him out – till he casts us out.

MOWGLI: Then, live a thousand years, Baloo. But – we have hunted greatly together, ye and I, and brothers are we till the end. There is one law for ye, and another for me, but the love between us shall bind us as strongly as that law.

BAGHEERA: Good hunting! We are thy people – we are still thy people. We will meet thee as of old among the thickets.

WOLVES: By the moonlight when thou art wearied of houses – by the still pools – on the high rocks under the stars.

BALOO: Oh, Lords of Life and Death, there has never been a wonder like this wonder! Give him the favour of the Jungle: – [*Beasts vanish.*]

Song

On the trails that thou must tread
To the thresholds of our dread
Where the flower blossoms red –
Through the nights when thou must lie
Prisoned from our mother sky,
Hearing us, thy loves, go by;
Wood and water, wind and tree,
Wisdom, strength, and courtesy,
Jungle favour go with thee.*

* The final part of 'The Outsong' at the end of 'The Spring Running' (*The Second Jungle Book*). This version is three lines shorter than that in the book (see Introduction, note 31) and contains several slight variants.

ACT IV. SCENE I

[MOWGLI *sits down:* DULIA *reclines with her head on his knee.*]

MOWGLI [*after thought*]: And from now, we tread a new trail — together.

DULIA [*sleepily, half lifting arms*]: What is it, beloved?

MOWGLI [*stooping above her. She throws her arms backward round* MOWGLI's *neck*]: It is this. [*Lips meet.*]

Textual Variants

The typescript of *The Jungle Play* is undated and carries no author's name. It runs to eighty-five pages, not numbered consecutively but with the page numbers starting afresh with each successive act and scene. Kipling has made deletions, additions, or revisions on fifty of the pages: no changes have been made in Act IV. The deletions are made with a brush and ink, the additions and corrections in pen and ink. On a few occasions early in the typescript, Kipling has made the correction with the same brush with which he made the deletion, instead of shifting to a pen.

PROLOGUE

1. *[confusedly] . . . notice us*: '(*confusedly*). Don't pinch! Stop pulling my tail! Good hunting, free people! Yah! They think themselves too fine to notice us.'

2 *Throw rubbish at them*: 'Let's throw rubbish at them.'

3 *What do the Free People?*: 'What are the Free People doing?'

4 *Look over . . . Free People!*: 'Looking over their dirty cubs. Phew! I wouldn't have a child like a wolf-cub, not for all the nuts in Seeonee.'

5 *Look and accept*: 'Look and accept them.'

6 *a Wolf*: 'any Wolf'.

7 *We have seen. We accept*: 'We have seen them. We accept them.'

8 *What is the creature*: 'What in the Jungle is the creature'.

9 *It will not stay very long*: 'It will not be here very long'.

10 *it was . . . he gave*: 'it was very thin and poor. The Lame Tiger gave'.

11 *He kills it to-night*: 'He will kill it to-night'.

12 *Shere Khan . . . came on*: 'Shere Khan was hunting man that night, and he came on'.

13 *brave; he followed*: 'brave, and he followed'.

14 *The man-child . . . fancy to it*: 'Yes, the man-child strayed right into Mother Wolf's cave and I suppose Mother Wolf took a fancy to it.' The sentences that followed have been deleted: 'And you know what she did? Mang the Bat heard it all!'

15 *She told . . . if he dared!*: 'She told Shere Khan that he might come inside and fight for the man cub if he dared!'

16 *knows that*: 'knows it!'

17 *Accept it, Wolves*: 'Accept it, O Wolves.'

18 *Let him die*: 'Let us kill him. Let him die.' The first of the sentences that follow was originally assigned to 'A Wolf' and the next to 'Wolves', but the names have been deleted and the whole of the speech given to 'Wolves'.

19 *Quiet, striped cattle-killer!*: 'Quiet, thou striped cattle-killer!'

20 *will*: 'can'.

21 *Do*: 'Will'.

22 *Jungle Law*: 'Law'.

23 *flesh eating*: 'killing'.

24 *man-cub; we need*: 'man-cub, but we need'.

25 *What is this . . . Free Hunters?*: 'What is this talk of training man-cubs to run with the Free Hunters?'

26 *thing*: 'brat'.

27 *Listen . . . we know him*: 'That is Bagheera – all over! Soft and quiet as a snake! As if all the Jungle didn't know him and fear him!'

28 *Bagheera*: 'He'.

29 *shame*: 'a shame'.

30 *full*: 'a full'.

31 *every night. Take the bull!*: 'every night. The Bull!'

32 *Let us*: 'Now let us'.

33 *And . . . call us greedy!*: The two sentences that followed have been deleted: 'Well, the man-cub will die sooner or later. He ought to have belonged to us.'

34 *Come . . . their bull*: 'Come along, and we'll make faces at them as they eat the bull.'

35 *well done*: 'well done, and quickly.'

36 *found it*: 'first met'.

37 *coat*: 'skin'.

38 *his pack look to it*: 'his friends beware!'

39 *Very well matched*: 'They are very well matched'.

ACT I

1 *Why . . . word*: 'Why did they not send me word and I would have hunted with them?'

2 *pull out*: 'remove'.

3 *man-paws*: 'clever man-paws'.

4 *hunt*: 'pack hunt'.

5 *Ah! . . . Grey Brother!*: 'Ah! Something is afoot. Good hunting!'

6 *Good hunting . . . because –*: 'Good hunting. I have come back to thee, Little Brother, because –'

7 *thee; do not hunt*: 'thee, but do not hunt'.

8 *Yes – sick chickens*: 'I know. A sick chicken'.

9 *friends*: 'warm friends'.

10 *opened*: 'torn'.

11 *What of it?*: The sentence that followed has been deleted: 'Shere Khan is all long tail and long talk, like Mao the peacock' (the phrase in Act II, Scene 1, and also in 'Mowgli's Brothers', is 'long tail and loud talk').

12 *ankle-bones. I chased*: 'bones, but I chased'.

13 *old*: 'very old'.

14 *buck. Then*: 'buck, and then'.

15 *That*: 'It' (no emphasis).

16 *Thou*: 'But thou'.

17 *What do I need of it?*: This sentence has been added in Kipling's hand.

18 *Thou*: 'But thou' (no emphasis on 'thou').

19 *dances inside them after dark*: 'dances inside after dark'.

20 *full gorge*: 'full and tale'.

21 *I am . . . Shere Khan*: This was originally two sentences: 'Man's cunning I know: and wolves' cunning I know, but this little Frog knows both. I do not think I would be in thy hide to-night, Shere Khan.' The first has been deleted and the new sentence runs on into the altered second sentence.

22 *garth*: 'work': the concluding three lines of the verse have been added to the typescript in Kipling's hand.

23 *millet again*: 'millet again, though I mended the fence with thorns only last night.'

24 *mend them*: 'help thee.'

25 *the way . . . our fruit*: 'the way the monkeys steal our fruit is simply scandalous.'

26 *We have to fight*: 'We have just to fight'.

27 *cow*: 'dun cow'.

28 *cow*: 'dun cow'.

29 *Art thou . . . them?*: The phrase that followed has been deleted: 'We need it.'

30 *[impatiently above pipe]*: '(*Impatiently*)'.

31 *wand*: 'poor wand'.

32 *gun*: 'very gun'.

33 *Jungle*: 'Jungle by night'.

34 *claws*: 'teeth'. The sentence that followed has been deleted: 'MOTHER WOLF. I remember how the old ape ran and roared.'

ACT II

1 *The grey ape . . . Jungle?*: The sentence that followed has been deleted: 'Why, our youngest cubs know *him*.'

2 *Bent – with white hair*: 'Bent, with whitest hair'.

3 *buffaloes*: 'village buffaloes'.

4 *I will . . . goat*: 'I will give him a young calf – (*hastily*) better perhaps, a goat. Yes, a goat'.

5 *the old gun –*: The phrase that followed has been deleted: 'the old shuffle.'

6 *Listen . . . Dulia*: The sentence that followed has been deleted: 'He is a master of word craft.'

7 *buffaloes*: 'village buffaloes'.

8 *with them*: 'with the buffaloes.'

9 *there's another of our bullocks dead*: 'there's another bullock's back broken!'

10 *poor*: 'bad'.

11 *bring*: 'take'.

12 *But this is for my enemies also*: 'But it is for my enemies.'

13 *The Jungle forbid*: 'The Gods of the Jungle forbid'.

14 *beast*: 'thing'.

15 *That is not fairy tale*: 'There, is not that a pretty fairy tale.'

16 *stupid*: 'fat stupid'.

17 *risk*: 'any risk'.

18 *trap*: 'man-trap'.

19 *call*: 'direct'.

20 *Let Rama the herd-bull lead*: 'Let the herd-bull lead'.

21 *charge thee all down the ravine*: 'charge thee into the plain.'

22 *Send . . . the bulls*: 'Send a brother to the left flank.'

23 *What is it?*: This sentence has been added in Kipling's hand.

24 *smoke him*: 'tree him'.

25 *even a jest*: 'even worth that'.

26 *Get to cover, and*: 'Get to cover. I will hide too, and'.

27 *[Brings down gun.]*: The two sentences that followed have been deleted: 'Money and a new reputation. I need them both.'

28 *It is . . . Jungle-brat*: 'It is beyond all endurance. A boy without caste or courtesy – '.

29 *hunter*: 'bold hunter'.

30 MOWGLI: The phrase that followed has been deleted: 'Without caste or courtesy.'

31 *the hand of the Little White One*: 'the hand of my foster-mother and the Little White One'.

32 *Only another time*: 'Another time'.

33 *With those evil eyes shining?*: 'With that head – and those evil eyes?'

34 *Go*: 'Now, go'.

35 *Go in peace, Buldeo*: The passage that followed has been deleted: 'and the next time when thou tellest thy hunting tales to the villagers, do not be angry when I laugh, for I too am something of a hunter, and'.

36 *And I'll show*: 'And maybe also I'll show'.

37 *hunting there*: 'hunting'.

38 *What . . . another go?*: The words that followed have been deleted: 'who is more to be feared? He has man's cunning.'

39 *[Laughs.]*: The sentence that followed has been deleted: 'That is certain.'

40 *intoning a prayer*: The stage direction that followed has been deleted: '*This should be rather effective.*'

41 *one who . . . good*: 'one who does no harm!'

42 *wizard*: 'pestilent wizard'.

43 *mean to*: 'will'.

44 *Let me go to him!*: 'Let me go!'

45 *Listen, man folk!*: 'Hark ye, children of men!'

46 *I have stolen none of them*: 'Ye will find I have stolen none of them'.

47 *alone*: 'alone in the Jungle'.

ACT III

1 *the great bulls trample him flat*: 'the great bulls blunder through the ravine and trample him flat'.

2 *alone*: 'alone hence forth'.

3 *restless pack*: 'uneasy pack'.

4 *thy teeth on my thigh still*: 'thy teeth here still'.

5 *Akela! Bring me the head!*: 'Akela! The head!'

6 *I have not heard*: 'I do not hear'.

7 *eyes in the dark*: 'eyes on the grass'.

8 *Oh I forgot*: 'Oh yes. I forgot.'

9 *moonrise*: 'the moon rises'.

10 *trail of men*: 'custom of men'. Kipling has first changed 'men' to 'man' and then substituted 'custom of men'.

11 *By whose . . . Shere Khan?*: 'For that little matter, by whose leave did I kill Shere Khan yonder?'

12 *senseless*: 'ye senseless'.

13 *Didst thou . . . my life?*: 'Didst thou give *me* up when Shere Khan sought *my* life?'

14 *I – I am thy Lair-Mother*: 'I – I love thee. I am thy Lair Mother.'

15 *Free Hunters – my brothers!*: The sentence that followed has been deleted: 'Are ye not a little ashamed?'

16 *next*: 'on'.

17 *They are mine and thine*: 'I am between thee and them.'

18 *through the . . . thy Jungle*: 'through *thy* jungle'.

19 *I will take . . . village*: 'I will take a price from the village such as man has never taken'.

20 *[picks up her hands]*: '(*Picks up her hands and grits teeth*)'.

21 *My Lord, I believe*: 'I believe – my Lord.'

22 *Grey Brother . . . hither*: The sentence that followed has been deleted: 'There is big hunting afoot.'

23 *Now, Hathi . . . man-pack*: The sentence that followed has been deleted: 'I will have no truce with them.'

24 *no truce with them*: 'no truce'. The sentence that followed has been deleted: 'I killed Shere Khan only because he wished to kill me.'

25 *her*: 'her' (no emphasis).

26 *men*: 'women'.

27 *I am . . . trail now*: The passage that followed has been deleted: 'He is wrath with his man-pack. Oh, woe! Woe! For the man-pack!'

28 *very*: 'very' (no emphasis).

29 *villagers. They*: 'villagers and they'.

30 *servants*: 'servants here'.

31 *in that village . . . one thing*: 'in that village one thing'.

32 *There . . . Red Flower*: The sentence that followed has been deleted: 'They shall lie out in the dew as I have lain; they shall sleep in the high grass as I have slept.'

33 *That shall . . . Hathi!*: The speech that followed has been deleted: 'BAL. Aah! And this is the naked thing I spoke for in the wolf-pack, when all the world was young!'

34 *WOLVES*: The sentence that followed has been deleted: 'There has been no hunting like this in all our time.'

35 *MOWGLI*: The sentence that followed has been deleted: 'They shall run as thy men ran from the fields ye reaped: till the bitter Karela grows over their roofs, and the wild pig root in their streets, till Bagheera and I lie down in the temple and the buck drink at their tanks.'

36 *Lest*: 'But lest'.

37 *and their water-tanks*: This phrase has been added in Kipling's hand.

38 *Only the . . . taint*: The sentence that followed has been deleted: 'It burns in my mouth now.'

39 *that traps and wounds women*: 'that traps women and wounds maidens'.

40 *And Dulia*: 'Our daughter'.

41 *In the Jungle by night?*: 'In the Jungle?'

42 *If I reach . . . cooking-pots*: The sentence that followed has been deleted: 'I shall bring such a lawsuit against the village as shall eat it to the bone.'

READ MORE IN PENGUIN

In every corner of the world, on every subject under the sun, Penguin represents quality and variety – the very best in publishing today.

For complete information about books available from Penguin – including Puffins, Penguin Classics and Arkana – and how to order them, write to us at the appropriate address below. Please note that for copyright reasons the selection of books varies from country to country.

In the United Kingdom: Please write to *Dept. EP, Penguin Books Ltd, Bath Road, Harmondsworth, West Drayton, Middlesex UB7 ODA*

In the United States: Please write to *Consumer Sales, Penguin Putnam Inc., P.O. Box 12289 Dept. B, Newark, New Jersey 07101-5289.* VISA and MasterCard holders call 1-800-788-6262 to order Penguin titles

In Canada: Please write to *Penguin Books Canada Ltd, 10 Alcorn Avenue, Suite 300, Toronto, Ontario M4V 3B2*

In Australia: Please write to *Penguin Books Australia Ltd, P.O. Box 257, Ringwood, Victoria 3134*

In New Zealand: Please write to *Penguin Books (NZ) Ltd, Private Bag 102902, North Shore Mail Centre, Auckland 10*

In India: Please write to *Penguin Books India Pvt Ltd, 11 Community Centre, Panchsheel Park, New Delhi 110017*

In the Netherlands: Please write to *Penguin Books Netherlands bv, Postbus 3507, NL-1001 AH Amsterdam*

In Germany: Please write to *Penguin Books Deutschland GmbH, Metzlerstrasse 26, 60594 Frankfurt am Main*

In Spain: Please write to *Penguin Books S. A., Bravo Murillo 19, 1° B, 28015 Madrid*

In Italy: Please write to *Penguin Italia s.r.l., Via Benedetto Croce 2, 20094 Corsico, Milano*

In France: Please write to *Penguin France, Le Carré Wilson, 62 rue Benjamin Baillaud, 31500 Toulouse*

In Japan: Please write to *Penguin Books Japan Ltd, Kaneko Building, 2-3-25 Koraku, Bunkyo-Ku, Tokyo 112*

In South Africa: Please write to *Penguin Books South Africa (Pty) Ltd, Private Bag X14, Parkview, 2122 Johannesburg*

READ MORE IN PENGUIN

Published or forthcoming:

The Chrysalids John Wyndham

Genetic mutation has devastated the world. In the primitive society that has emerged from its ruins, any sign of deviation is ruthlessly hunted out and destroyed. David lives in fear of discovery, for he is part of a secret group who are able to communicate with each other through their thoughts. As they grow older they feel increasingly isolated. Then one of them marries a 'norm' with terrifying consequences.

The Waves Virginia Woolf

The Waves traces the lives of a group of friends from childhood to youth and middle age. While social events, individual achievements and disappointments form its narrative, the novel is most remarkable for the poetic language that conveys the inner life of its characters: their aspirations, their triumphs and regrets, their awareness of unity and isolation.

Heart of Darkness Joseph Conrad

In Conrad's haunting tale Marlow, a seaman and wanderer, recounts his journey to the heart of Africa in search of the enigmatic Kurtz. He discovers how Kurtz has gained his position of power over the local people, and radically questions not only his own nature and values, but those of his society. '*Heart of Darkness* seemed to reach into the heart of Conrad himself' Peter Ackroyd, *The Times*

The Garden Party and Other Stories Katherine Mansfield

Innovative, startlingly perceptive and aglow with colour, these fifteen stories were written towards the end of Katherine Mansfield's short life. Many are set in the author's native New Zealand, others in England and the French Riviera. All are revelations of the unspoken, half-understood emotions that make up everyday experience.

BY THE SAME AUTHOR

'For my own part I worshipped Kipling at thirteen, loathed him at seventeen, enjoyed him at twenty, despised him at twenty-five, and now again rather admire him. The one thing that was never possible, if one had read him at all, was to forget him' George Orwell

Just So Stories

Kipling's bewitching stories conjure up distant lands, the beautiful gardens of splendid palaces, the sea, the desert, and the jungle and its beasts. Inspired by Kipling's natural empathy with the animal world and by his obvious delight in human foibles and eccentricities, these strikingly imaginative fables explore a range of subjects from the animals themselves to the origins of things. The stories are linked by poems and scattered with Kipling's illustrations, which, intriguingly, contain hidden jokes and puzzles. *Just So Stories* was written for children, but the book transcends the boundaries of age and is of equal appeal to adults.

'Kipling is thrilling ... every story is somehow, somewhere, touched with authentic magic' Peter Levi

Kim

Kipling's epic rendition of the imperial experience in India is also his greatest long work. Kim, a boy growing into early manhood and the lama, an old ascetic priest – are fired by a quest. Kim is white, a sahib, although born in India. While he wants to play the Great Game of Imperialism, he is also spiritually bound to the lama and he tries to reconcile these opposing strands. The lama, meanwhile, searches for redemption from the Wheel of Life. A celebration of their friendship in an often hostile environment, *Kim* captures the opulence of India's exotic landscape, overlaid by the uneasy presence of the British Raj.

'Extraordinary ... the British Empire's *Huckleberry Finn*' Barbara Trapido

BY THE SAME AUTHOR

'The most complete man of genius I have ever known' Henry James

The Jungle Books

Mowgli, the man-cub who is brought up by wolves in the jungles of Central India, is one of the greatest literary myths ever created. As he embarks on a series of thrilling escapades, Mowgli encounters such unforgettable creatures as Bagheera, the graceful black panther, and Shere Khan, the tiger with the blazing eyes. Other animal stories range from the simple heroism found in 'Rikki-tikki-tavi' to the macabre comedy 'The Undertakers'. A rich and complex fable of human life, Kipling's enduring classic dazzles the imagination with its astonishing descriptive powers and lively sense of adventure.

'Kipling is the most sophisticated, most devilishly complicated short-story writer this country has ever produced' William Boyd

Also published:

Plain Tales from the Hills
Puck of Pook's Hill
Selected Stories
Selected Poems